MW01295353

Lucy's
Nauvoo

EDITED BY RONALD E. ROMIG

John Whitmer Books
2009

For Lucy

Lucy's Nauvoo
Edited by Ronald E. Romig
Copy edited by Lavina Fielding Anderson
Thanks to: Anne Romig, artwork; Rene Romig, draft and proofing; Erin Jennings, Mary Ann Hubbard reminiscence and *The Cleveland Herald*; Lee and Marion Updike, Miss F. J., "Visit to Nauvoo;" LDS Church Library, sources and visual materials as noted.

John Whitmer Books, Independence, Missouri
JohnWhitmerBooks.com

Published in the United States of America
Copyright © 2009 by Ronald E. Romig
18 Oak Hill Cluster
Independence, MO 64057
rromig1@comcast.net

Without limiting the rights under copyright reserved above, no part of this publication may be reproduced, stored in, or introduced into a retrieval system, or transmitted, in any form or by any means (electronic, mechanical, photocopying, recording or otherwise), without the prior written permission of the publisher.

Images, unless otherwise cited, are the copyrighted intellectual property of and provided courtesy of Community of Christ Archives, [abbreviated CofC Archives], 1001 W. Walnut, Independence, MO 64050-3562

Cover, interior design, and maps by John Hamer
FRONT COVER IMAGE: Lucy Mack Smith painting, CofC Archives.
BACK COVER IMAGE: View of Nauvoo, J. W. Gunnison, *The Mormons, or, Latter-Day Saints* (Philadelphia, PA: J. B. Lippincott & Co., 1860), frontispiece.

This volume is heavily based upon the citational roadmap provided by Lavina Fielding Anderson of Lucy's Nauvoo experiences, in "Epilogue: Lucy's Last Years," *Lucy's Book: A Critical Edition of Lucy Mack Smith's Family Memoir* (Signature Books, 2001).

Table *of* Contents

Original spellings have been retained in quoted sources.

Lucy's Nauvoo

Sketch of Lucy Mack Smith drawn by Anne Romig, based on photograph, (see page 103), and the pattern from Lucy's oilcloth tablecloth design.

Brief Biography *of* Lucy Mack Smith

by Vida Elizabeth Smith, Lucy's Great-grandaughter

GATHERED FROM her own writings, the writings of others, and reminiscences of her personal acquaintances, the character of Lucy Mack Smith appeals to one as more than ordinary in interest and strength. She possessed a peculiar endowment, viewed from the stand-point of heredity and environment. Born [in 1875] in hardy old New England, Gilsum, Cheshire County, New Hampshire, of parents full of fire and fealty of revolutionary days, and [growing up] while the echoes of the glad-sounding independence bell were still vibrant on the warm July air, hers was a spiritual heritage of freedom. Within her very soul was a magnificent appreciation of liberty. She felt the quickening pulse of the nation newly baptized with freedom, and it thrilled her with a love for humanity and faith in God. The abhorrence of domination and kingly power was manifest in her by the hatred of all oppression, a love of justice, but a conscientious firmness in the performance of what she deemed right. She was not a large woman, but her own valuation of manhood and womanhood, and their wonderful opportunities, coupled with an approachable and softened dignity, placed her on a little elevation that even those who remember her but slightly, recall. Her eyes were keen, clear, and blue, and even in old age did not require glasses.

She was the youngest child of a large family of sons and daughters. While quite young her mother, thinking she was about to die, gave her to her brother, Stephen Mack. However, the mother recovered, and Lucy lived on at home, sometimes favored above the rest, sometimes a little burden-bearer; as in the case of her older sister, who was ill for three years. During much of the later days of her affliction, Lucy had the sole care of her day and night. She even carried the emaciated body in her frail young arms, although the careful little nurse was but thirteen years of age. Her highly sensitive spirit breaks forth in an agony of remembrance, years later, at the painful incident that always accompanied this picture. Her hand having slipped she hurt the invalid, who cried, "Oh, sister, you hurt me."

Tunbridge, Vermont.

After the death of this sister, her brother took her with him to his home in Tunbridge, Vermont. He found the constant attendance upon the sick, meeting death often, and the comfort given by the severe religious creeds of that day, had made her melancholy and sad. This brother was in youth a courageous and daring soldier, but now placidly settled in business. Lucy found life pleasanter, and grew brighter and more optimistic. Here she met her gentle-voiced lover, Joseph Smith, for the first time, and here, upon her second visit to her brother, she was married in the month of January, 1796.

The thrift and forethought shown by her in laying by the wedding gift of one thousand dollars, given by the brother and his partner, would appear to be the effect of home training. She was a woman of impulse and determined in action. She spoke by nature authoritatively and wisely. Her mother was a woman of culture and refinement, and gave to this daughter, by grace of birth, the great gift of language.

From the father came the innate power of command, softened and made gentle, but it was there with a strength of character and womanly force to support it. From that [what?] liberty thrilled somewhere came the love for humanity, and delight in God's word. She had a high, fine sense of imagination, which in later life, quickened by the Spirit, developed the gift of prophecy and vision, born of hope and faith.

It was under these inspirations, and with these natural graces that she made the celebrated prophecies while passing from Buffalo, New

York, to Kirtland, Ohio, and in a measure took control of the chaotic condition on the boat, and brought forth order and inspired hope. This also is apparent in the visit made by her to Pontiac, Michigan.

How often in her youth when almost carried into excesses of religious excitement did the gentle but sometimes suddenly firm spirit of her adored husband meet her soul with some cooling, cautioning word. She accepted and was kept from the maelstrom of religious fanaticism that was sucking down the souls of men in that time. How quickly she rallied to the boy by her side in his struggles for light, and how she threw her life into the channel of his when the angel's message came! Every hope and fear was engulfed in a great wave of enthusiasm, that never lessened, for the triumph of truth and the upbuilding of the church of God. Well fitted to be mother of men destined to be leaders in a religious movement such as she saw her sons leading, her courage and zeal, her unwavering faith sustained, and her splendid determination was like a reservoir of strength to them, as many facts in her life's history would justify us in believing,

She possessed a high sense of duty and her standard of morals was unsurpassed. Perhaps there was a touch of the iron of old New York, to Kirtland, Ohio, and in a England sometimes in her rebukes. Sometimes the rigidity of her discipline of self and others looked severe, but it was not without its affectionate sequence, love of man, and love of right. Hers was a mission of service wherever she went; a nurse, a comforter, a counselor; wise, discreet, and sympathetic. A woman of action, sensitive to the necessity for immediate proceedings, she sometimes took weighty matters in her own hands, as in the case of the school and meetinghouse building in Kirtland. . . .

Joseph Smith Sr., painting by Henry Inouye Jr., 1997, courtesy Helen Inouye. Joseph Sr. never fully recovered from the trauma he experienced as a result of the expulsion from Missouri during the winter of 1838-39.

One can trace her impulsiveness by many acts, but, too, she was self[less]-centered, conscientious, fearless, and determined. Hospitable and charitable, her magnificent spirit was afflicted by the afflictions of others as she passed with the family and church through their weary wanderings to Nauvoo. There she nursed her husband in his last illness, during which he paid her a beautiful tribute of appreciation upon his peaceful, love-lighted deathbed. . . .

She laid him away in the cemetery by the grand old river. She thought that separation the height and depth of all calamity. . . . Bravely she walked with that unflinching courage and redoubtable faith back to her lonely home, which is still standing under the brow of the hill at Nauvoo.

Months passed; a son and grandchildren went to the little burying ground to sleep. Abuse and persecution kept her other sons almost in exile. She swept for the last time her own hearthstone, and yielding to loving importunities she went to live and die within the home of her son Joseph. Here sickness came upon her, but she lived to record the goodness of those who cared for her, and to be a helpless, but not a hopeless, invalid. The indomitable will was unbroken. As graciously she sat in her chair, wheeled about by grandchildren, as she had stood in testimony of the truth in other days. With as much dignity she wore the flesh in weakness as she had worn it in its freshness and beauty.

At last came that rose-scented day in June when every other sorrow and indignity sank into nothingness. She had them take her to the great sunlighted dining-room, to the side of her two murdered sons, Hyrum and Joseph. Ah, she did not falter even here. She proclaimed afterwards, "My heart was thrilled with

Lucy Mack Smith, painting by Henry Inouye Jr., 1997, courtesy Helen Inouye. Lucy's urging for building a church meetinghouse at Kirtland, Ohio, ultimately influenced the outcome of the Kirtland Temple.

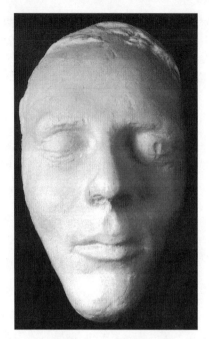 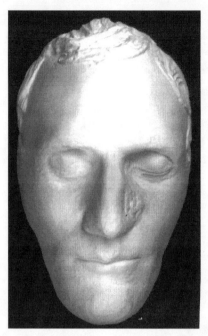

Joseph Smith Jr., and Hyrum Smith death masks, courtesy Church Archives, The Church of Jesus Christ of Latter-day Saints.

grief and indignation; the blood curdled in my veins." But she was self-poised and strong even there, in her old age, with bone of her bone and flesh of her flesh lying cold and silent before her. Rispah—nay, not that! A true American Latter Day Saint mother, she hears even there that still, comforting voice, "I have taken them unto myself."

To-day there are waste places where stood the great square dining-room where she looked upon her slain, but her testimony comes to us strong with heart-beats of a noble and beautiful spirit. Though she drained a bitter cup to the dregs,

there is not one note of weakness in her recital. Even in that supreme moment when memory lashed her grief-sick soul, reason reigned. Calmly she turned from the lifeless forms whereon was set the price of heartless men, to the solicitous anxiety for another son, a victim of persecution who died in less than six weeks. She never forgot the men who had wrought so much bitterness in her life.

Quietly she spent her last days in the sunny room still open to the sunbeams from the south, in the old Mansion House. Wise in conversation and firm in opinion as when she moved quickly and with power to the accomplishment of some youthful impulse. In May, 1855 [sic], just eleven years after that tragic June day, she fell asleep . . . leaving the record of one who loved much, suffered much, and was ever loyal. A woman who had adhered to her own affectionately rigid rules in rearing her family, and held the undying love of husband, children, and grandchildren. One who inspired reverence and confidence, though speaking directly and plainly, the memory of her is of a character strong, fearless, clear-minded, and God-fearing.

–Vida Elizabeth Smith, "Character Sketch of Lucy Mack Smith," *Journal of History* 1, no. 4 (October 1908): 406-12.

Detail of an oilcloth painted by Lucy in New York, courtesy L. Tom Perry Special Collections, H. B. Lee Library, BYU.

Heman C. Smith, an RLDS Church Historian, observed:

AS LIGHTS AND shadows enter into the formation of a picture, so virtues and vices of parents enter into the characters of men and women, and it was the Mack character as developed in Lucy mingled with the Smith character that produced the historic characters so well known in connection with the great church movement of which the world has had so much to say.

This combination resulted in the production of the courageous, aggressive, and yet high moral character of Joseph and Don Carlos, the milder, yet as firm and true, character of Alvin, Hyrum, Samuel, Sophron[i]a, and Lucy, and the determined and sometimes defiant character developed in William and Catherine [Katherine in later sources]—noble characters all. Other elements entering from generation to generation present to the student of character the kaleidoscopic picture now presented by the Smith family.

–Heman C. Smith, "Distinguished Women: Lucy Mack Smith," *Journal of History* 12, no. 1 (January 1919): 106-09.

A Nauvoo Setting

We pick up the thread of Lucy's life well toward its end, leaving the narration of the forepart of her fascinating story to others. We first encounter Lucy shortly after the Latter Day Saints' forced expulsion from the State of Missouri. Mother Smith, her husband Joseph Smith Senior, and others of her family and friends now found refuge in Illinois. The Latter Day Saints as a whole were beginning to recover from the effects of exposure to winter during their journey out of Missouri. Lucy's sons, Joseph and Hyrum, only recently joined their families in Illinois, having been incarcerated in the jails of Missouri. Joseph Smith Jr. sought a place where followers of this new American religion could gather together again and rebuild their religion and their lives. Joseph selected a struggling village known as Commerce, along the Illinois side of a beautiful bend of the Mississippi River.

When the Smith Family arrived at Commerce, Illinois, soon to be known as Nauvoo, Joseph Jr. moved his family into a rudely built two story block house (of squared off logs), with one room down stairs and one upstairs. The building had once been the location of an agency for the Sac Indian tribe. It came to be known as "the Homestead." This tiny space served as home for the family, and where Joseph conducted Church business.

The first winter, the summer kitchen at the back corner of the house provided lodging for Joseph Sr., and Lucy Mack Smith. Nauvoo would become Lucy's home for most of the rest of her life.

–Julia Murdock Smith Dixon Middleton (1831-1880), Joseph Smith, Jr. Family Organization, Website: http://www.josephsmith-jr.com/julia.htm.

Joseph Smith III recalled that his grandparents later moved into a double log house located on the northwest corner of the block containing the Nauvoo House.

–Richard P. Howard, ed., *The Memoirs of President Joseph Smith III (1832-1914)* (Independence, Missouri: Herald Publishing House, 1978), 5.

Original spellings have been retained in quoted sources.

The Joseph Smith Homestead, Nauvoo, Illinois, drawing by Henry Inouye, Jr., courtesy Helen Inouye.

Wandle Mace

Wandle Mace was living near Commerce, Illinois, when the Saints began to gather there in 1839. Mace became acquainted with the entire Smith family shortly after their arrival. Wandle recalled,

ALMOST AS SOON AS the Father and Mother of the Prophet Joseph Smith set their feet upon the hospitable shore of Illinois, I became acquainted with them. I frequently visited them and listened with intense interest as they related the history of the rise of the church in every detail. With tears, they could not control, they narrated the scenes they had passed through.

–Wandle Mace, Autobiography, ca. 1890, Holograph, MS 1189, 33, LDS Church Library.

Parley P. Pratt Recollection

Parley Pratt, another early Church leader, had also been incarcerated in Missouri. The Smith family was just beginning to settle into their new homes at Nauvoo when Parley P. Pratt arrived from Missouri on July 11, 1839, seven days after his escape from jail. Parley provides a glimpse of Lucy soon after the family settled at Nauvoo:

Parley P. Pratt.

Here I met brother Joseph Smith, from whom I had been separated since the close of the mock trial in Richmond the year previous. Neither of us could refrain from tears as we embraced each other once more as free men. . . . He blessed me with a warmth of sympathy and brotherly kindness which I shall never forget. Here also I met with Hyrum Smith and many others of my fellow prisoners with a glow of mutual joy and satisfaction which language will never reveal. Father and Mother Smith, the parents of our Prophet and President, were also overwhelmed with tears of joy and congratulation; wept like children as they took me by the hand; but O, how different from the tears of bitter sorrow which were pouring down their cheeks as they gave us the parting hand in Far West, and saw us dragged away by fiends in human form.

–Scot and Maurine Proctor, eds., Parley P. Pratt, *Autobiography of Parley P. Pratt* (Salt Lake City, Utah: Deseret Book, 2000), 354-55.

Death *of* Joseph Smith Sr.

Joseph Sr. and Lucy were in Nauvoo less than a year when Joseph began to grow ill. Old age and the cumulative effects of exposure to winter weather during the expulsion from Missouri took a heavy toll on his health.

Shortly before his death, Joseph Sr. called his family together for a blessing. He comforted Lucy saying, "Mother, do you not know, that you are one of the most singular women in the world. . . ? You have brought up all my children, and could always comfort them when I could not. We have often wished that we might both die at the same time, but you must not desire to die when I do, for you must stay to comfort the children when I am gone. Do not mourn, but try to be comforted. Your last days shall be your best days."

–Richard Van Wagoner and Steven Walker, *A Book of Mormons* (Salt Lake City, Utah: Signature Books, 1982), 311-12.

ON THE 14th of September 1840, after blessing his children individually Joseph Sr. "closed his earthly career. Mother Smith felt this bereavement keenly."

–James Linforth, ed., *Route from Liverpool to Great Salt Lake Valley* (Liverpool, England: F. D. Richards, 1855), 71.

Joseph Smith III remembered that his grandfather "died while they were living in the double log house on the east side of Main Street."

–Richard P. Howard, ed., *The Memoirs of President Joseph Smith III (1832-1914)*, 5.

William Smith expressed his thoughts about the loss of his father in a letter to his friend William W. Phelps.

IT IS NOT Nauvoo! for . . . there lie the silver locks of an aged and martyred father, martyred by a Missouri persecution, in the grave, numbered with the dead. Yet Nauvoo contains almost all that is dear to me. My poor old mother, almost worn out with years and trouble, and three sisters that remain.

–William Smith, Letter to William W. Phelps, November 10, 1844, Bordentown, New Jersey, *The Prophet* 1, no. 27 (November 23, 1844): 3.

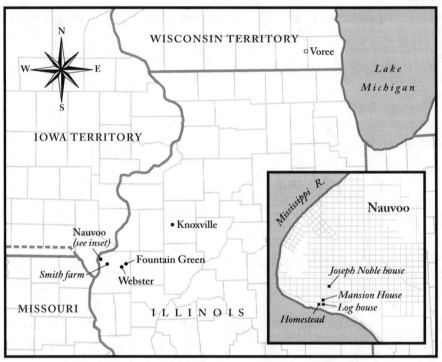

Locations of Lucy's Illinois residences, 1839-56. Map by John Hamer.

EGYPTIAN PARCHMENTS

Formerly, while headquartered at Kirtland, Ohio, the Church acquired several Egyptian scrolls and four mummies from a traveling showman. These rarities proved to be not only a source of curiosity but eventually the basis of Joseph Smith Jr.'s Book of Abraham.

Throughout the Nauvoo period, Lucy served as caretaker of these interesting relics. Joseph provided a small house for his parents near the Homestead. Lucy moved the Egyptian artifacts to the upstairs chamber of this house, where she actively exhibited them for a small fee and bore her testimony to enquiring visitors. This provided Lucy a source of income.

A Fac-Simile from the Book of Abraham.

No. 2.

EXPLANATION OF THE ABOVE CUT.

Fig. 1. Kolob, signifying the first creation, nearest to the celestial, or the residence of God. First in government, the last pertaining to the measurement of time. The measurement, according to celestial time; which, celestial time, signifies one day to a cubit. One day, in Kolob, is equal to a thousand years, according to the measurement of this earth, which is called by the Egyptians Jah-oh-eh.

Fig. 2. Stands next to Kolob, called by the Egyptians Oliblish, which is the next grand governing creation, near to the celestial or the place where God resides; holding the key of power also, pertaining to other planets; as revealed from God to Abraham, as he offered sacrifice upon an altar, which he had built unto the Lord.

Fig. 3. Is made to represent God, sitting upon his throne, clothed with power and authority: with a crown of eternal light upon his head: representing, also, the grand Key-Words of the Holy Priest-hood, as revealed to Adam in the Garden of Eden, as also to Seth, Noah, Melchisedeck, Abraham, and all to whom the Priesthood was revealed.

Fig. 4. Answers to the Hebrew word raukeeyang, signifying expanse, or the firmament of the heavens; also, a numerical figure, in Egyptian, signifying one thousand; answering to the measuring of the time of Oliblish, which is equal with Kolob in its revolution and in its measuring of time.

Fig. 5. Is called in Egyptian Enish-go-on-dosh; that is one of the governing planets also; and is said by the Egyptians to be the Sun, and to borrow its light from Kolob through the medium of Kae-e-vanrash, which is the grand Key, or in other words, the governing power, which governs fifteen other fixed planets or stars, as also Floeese or the Moon, the Earth and the Sun in their annual revolutions. This planet receives its power through the medium of Kli-flos-is-es, or Hah-ko-kau-beam, the stars represented by numbers 22, and 23, receiving light from the revolutions of Kolob.

Fig. 6. Represents this earth in its four quarters.

Fig. 7. Represents God sitting upon his throne, revealing, through the heavens, the grand Key-Words of the Priesthood; as, also, the sign of the Holy Ghost unto Abraham, in the form of a dove.

Fig. 8. Contains writing that cannot be revealed unto the world; but is to be had in the Holy Temple of God.

Fig. 9. Ought not to be revealed at the present time.

Fig. 10. Also.

Fig. 11. Also.—If the world can find out these numbers, So let it be, Amen.

Figures 12, 13, 14, 15, 16, 17, 18, 19, and 20, will be given in the own due time of the Lord.

The above translation is given as far as we have any right to give, at the present time.

Facsimile from Egyptian papyrus, as published in *Pearl of Great Price*, 1851.

Henry Caswall, April 1842

Henry Caswall's self caricature, 1842.

On April 18, 1842, Henry Caswall, an Episcopalian minister from Kemper College at St. Louis, Missouri, visited Nauvoo. While there, Caswall viewed the Egyptian parchments that Joseph Smith used for the Book of Abraham. When Caswall asked to also see the four accompanying Egyptian mummies, he was escorted to Lucy Smith's small house where the mummies were stored upstairs. Caswell described the mummies and his conversation with Mother Smith:

I WALKED OVER TO the store, where the storekeeper expressed his readiness to show me the mummies. Accordingly he led the way to a small house, the residence of the prophet's mother. On entering the dwelling, I was introduced to this eminent personage as a traveler ... desirous of seeing the wonders of Nauvoo. She welcomed me to the holy city, and told me that here I might see what great things the Lord had done for his people. "I am old," she said, "and I shall soon stand before the judgment-seat of Christ; but what I say to you now, I would say on my death-bed. My son Joseph has had revelations from God since he was a boy, and he is indeed a true prophet of Jehovah. The angel of the Lord appeared to him fifteen years since, and shewed him the cave where the original golden plates of the book of Mormon were deposited. He shewed him also the Urim and Thummun, by which he might understand the meaning of the inscriptions on the plates, and he shewed him the golden breastplate of the high priesthood. My son received these precious gifts, he interpreted the holy record, and now the believers in that revelation are more than a hundred thousand in number.

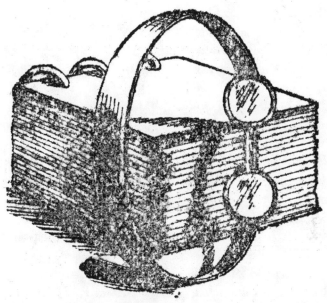

SPECTACLES AND PLATES

Depiction of Book of Mormon plates.

I have myself seen and handled the golden plates; they are about eight inches long, and six wide; some of them are sealed together and are not to be opened, and some of them are loose. They are all connected by a ring which passes through a hole at the end of each plate, and are covered with letters beautifully engraved. I have seen and felt also the Urim and Thummim. They resemble two large bright diamonds set in a bow like a pair of spectacles. My son puts these over his eyes when he reads unknown languages, and they enable him to interpret them in English. I have likewise carried in my hands the sacred breastplate. It is composed of pure gold, and is made to fit the breast very exactly." While the old woman was thus delivering herself, I fixed my eyes steadily upon her. She faltered, and seemed unwilling to meet my glance, but gradually recovered her self-possession. The melancholy thought entered my mind that this poor old creature was not simply a dupe of her son's knavery, but that she had taken an active part in the deception. Several

English and American women were in the room, and seemed to treat her with profound veneration. . . . She then directed me up a steep flight of stairs into a chamber, and slowly crept up after me. She showed me a wretched cabinet, in which were four naked mummies frightfully disfigured, and in fact most disgusting relics of mortality. "One (she said) was a king of Egypt, whom she named, two were his wives, and the remaining one was the daughter of another king." I asked her by what means she became acquainted with the names and histories of these mummies. She replied, "that her son had obtained this knowledge through the mighty power of God."

This lady seems to be an important aid in Joseph Smith's designs. She has revelations also.

—Henry Caswall, *The City of the Mormons; or Three Days at Nauvoo in 1842* (London: Printed for J. G. F. & J. Rivington, 1842), 26-27.

In Nauvoo Lucy's house was often filled with needy Saints. "Many of the sick owed the preservation of their lives to her motherly care, attention, and skill in nursing them, which she did without pecuniary consideration and the extent of which can only be appreciated by those who are personally acquainted with the dreadful scenes of sickness and distress, in consequence of the Missouri expulsion."

– Van Wagoner and Walker, *A Book of Mormons*, 311.

Reconstructed Joseph and Lucy house.

Female Relief Society, 1842

In 1842, a small group of women organized a sewing society at the home of Sarah M. Granger Kimball in Nauvoo to assist men working on the Church's temple. Joseph Smith proposed an alternative organization of the sisters "after a pattern of the priesthood." Joseph called the Female Relief Society of Nauvoo to order with twenty women present at its first meeting on March 17, 1842. Emma Smith and two counselors were set apart by priesthood leaders by the laying on of hands. The society incorporated women into the formal structure of the Church and afforded them significant opportunities and authority. The organization quickly grew. With a primary purpose of "looking to the wants of the poor," the Relief Society also regulated moral reform, supported temple construction, and petitioned the governor of Illinois on Joseph Smith's behalf.

– "Story of the Organization of the Relief Society," 129; Janath R. Cannon and Jill Mulvay-Derr, Relief Society, http://www.light-planet.com/mormons/basic/organization/Relief_Society_EOM.htm, accessed January 1, 2009.

Lucy participated in the March 24, 1842, meeting of the Relief Society.

MOTHER LUCY SMITH arose and said she rejoiced in view of what was doing—as she came in and look'd upon the sisters it gave her feelings of deep interest—Wept—said she was advanc'd in years and could not stay long—hop'd the Lord would bless and aid the Society in feeding the hungry, clothing the naked—that her work was nearly done—felt to pray that the blessings of heaven might rest upon the Society. . . . Mother Lucy Smith said—this Institution is a good one—we must watch over ourselves—that she came into the church of Jesus Christ of Latter-day Saints to do good—to get good, and to get into the celestial kingdom. She said we must cherish one another, watch over one another, comfort one another and gain instruction, that we may all sit down in heaven together.

–Minutes of the Second Meeting of the Relief Society, March 24, 1842, 12, 13, LDS Church Library.

Sutcliffe Maudsley Profile

Profile of Lucy Mack Smith, drawn by Sutcliffe Maudsley, ca. 1842, courtesy Church Archives, The Church of Jesus Christ of Latter-day Saints.

Though frequently the subject of word descriptions, around 1842 Nauvoo artist, Sutcliffe Maudsley captured Lucy visually, seated in a rocking chair. Maudsley was born at Accrington, Lancashire, England, May 10, 1808. Sutcliffe grew up in the Accrington manufacturing district and learned to design patterns used in the manufacture of fabric. The family came into contact with Latter Day Saint missionaries after they moved to Lancashire. Mauds—ley, his wife Elizabeth Foxcroft, and six children converted to the church in 1840 and emigrated to the United States, arriving at Nauvoo in 1841. The Maudsleys resided in the poorer section of Nauvoo, about one half mile northwest of Joseph Smith's home. Maudsley attempted to support his family by gardening. Joseph befriended Sutcliffe and encouraged him to use his artistic skills. Representing himself as a "profilist," Maudsley produced drawings of many Nauvoo Saints, including the extended Smith family.

Testimony of Mother Lucy Smith

Lucy also testified to the sisters at the April 28, 1842, Relief Society meeting. Wilford Woodruff recorded Lucy's statement.

MOTHER SMITH ROSE & said she was glad the time had come that iniquity could be detected & reproach thrown off from the heads of the church. We came into the church to be saved that we may live in peace & sit down in the Kingdom of heaven. If we listen to, & circulate every evil report, we shall idly spend the time which should be appropriated to the reading of the scriptures, the Book of Mormon. We must remember the words of Alma pray much at morning, noon & evening, feed the poor &c. She said she was old. Could not meet with the society but few times more, & wished to leave her testimony that the book of mormon [sic] is the book of God. That Joseph Smith is a man of God, a prophet of the Lord set apart to lead the people. If we observe his words it will be well with us; if we live righteously on earth, it will be well with us in Eternity.

–Scott G. Kenney, ed., *Wilford Woodruff's Journal*, January 1, 1841-December 31, 1845 (Midvale, Utah: Signature Books, 1983), 2: 202-03.

With Joseph *and* Emma

Right after her husband's death, Lucy also lost her son Don Carlos (1816-1841) to malarial fever at the age of 25.

Lucy's losses affected her health. Though fiercely independent, Lucy yielded to Joseph's and Emma's coaxing and moved into the Homestead with them. Lucy recalled:

I BROKE UP house-keeping, and at Joseph's request, I took up my residence at his house. Soon after . . . I was taken very sick and was brought nigh unto death. For five nights in succession Emma never left me, but stood at my bedside all night long, at the end of which time she was overcome with fatigue and taken sick herself. Joseph then took her place and watched with me the five succeeding nights as faithfully as Emma had done. . . . I began to recover, and, in the course of a few weeks, I was able to walk about the house a little, and sit up during the day. I have hardly been able to go on foot further than across the street since.

–Lavina Fielding Anderson, *Lucy's Book: Critical Edition of Lucy Mack Smith's Family Memoir*, (Salt Lake City, UT: Signature Books, 2001), 733.

On August 31, 1843, Joseph and Emma moved out of the Homestead and into the newly constructed Nauvoo Mansion House. Lucy moved with them.

–Anderson, *Lucy's Book*, 203.

W. Aitken, 1843

W. Aitken, an Englishman traveling up the Mississippi River, visited Nauvoo in 1843. Aitken did not mention seeing Lucy but described the promotion of the Egyptian relics:

We now left the temple, grove, and wooden oxen to get a glimpse of the prophet and, reconnoitering about his house, I saw a board stuck up at the end on which was painted Egyptian mummies exhibited, and ancient records explained. Price

A sign with this wording hung outside of the Nauvoo Mansion House to attract visitors.

twenty-five cents. My purse and the distance I had to travel to England seemed to say I must husband the cents and stay curiosity. On inquiring what these mummies were I found they had been exhibited in the States, and purchased by the prophet. The only thing farther that I could learn about the mummies was that one portion of them was the "leg of Pharaoh's daughter," and as it was very questionable with me whether I should give twenty-five cents to see the whole living frame of Pharaoh's daughter, I felt uneasy about seeing the "leg."

–W. Aitken, *Journey Up the Mississippi River, from Its Mouth to Nauvoo, the City of the Latter-Day Saints* (Ashton-Under-Lyne: John Williamson, 1845), 35.

Charlotte Haven, 1843

Charlotte Haven, a non-Mormon resident of Nauvoo, reported seeing the Egyptian scrolls during her 1843 visit with Lucy Mack Smith:

We called on Joseph's mother. . . . Madame Smith's residence is a log house very near her son's. She opened the door and received us cordially. She is a motherly kind of woman of about sixty years. She receives a little pittance by exhibiting the mummies to strangers. When we asked to see them, she lit a candle and conducted us up a short, narrow stairway to a low, dark room under the roof. On one side were standing half a dozen mummies, to whom she introduced us, King Onitus and his royal household,—one she did not know. Then she took up what seemed to be a club wrapped in a dark cloth, and said, "This is the leg of Pharaoh's daughter, the one that saved Moses." Repressing a smile, I looked from the mummies to the old lady, but could detect nothing but earnestness and sincerity on her countenance. Then she turned to a long table, set her candlestick down, and opened a long roll of manuscript, saying it was "the writing of Abraham and Isaac, written in Hebrew and Sanscrit [sic]," and she read several minutes from it as if it were English. It sounded very much like passages from the Old Testament—and it might have been for anything we knew—but she said she read it through the inspiration of her son Joseph, in whom she seemed to have perfect confidence. Then in the same way she interpreted to us hieroglyphics from another roll. One was Mother Eve being tempted by the serpent, who—the

Details from parchment fragments in Lucy's possession.

serpent, I mean—was standing on the tip of his tail, which with his two legs formed a tripod, and had his head in Eve's ear. I said, "But serpents don't have legs." "They did before the fall," she asserted with perfect confidence.

The Judge slipped a coin in her hand which she received smilingly, with a pleasant, "Come again," as we bade her goodby[e].

–Charlotte Haven, "A Girl's Letters from Nauvoo," January 3, 1843, *The Overland Monthly* 6, no. 96 (December, 1890), 623-24.

The judge Charlotte mentioned was Sylvester Emmons, a resident of Nauvoo who later became one of the editors of the *Nauvoo Expositor.*

Jane Manning James, 1843

Jane Manning James (1822-1911), photo provided courtesy of Louis Duffy.

Wishing to gather with the Saints, Jane and her family took a canal boat to Buffalo, New York. At Buffalo, they were denied passage on a ship to Nauvoo and made the 800-mile trek on foot. From 1843 to 1844, Jane worked in Joseph's and Emma's home. The Smith family moved into the new Nauvoo Mansion House around 1843. Jane described a memorable encounter with Mother Smith while working there.

I HAD TO PASS through Mother Smith's room to get to mine, [and] she would often stop me and talk to me. She told me all Brother Joseph's troubles, and what he had suffered in publishing the Book of Mormon. One morning I met Brother Joseph coming out of his mother's room. He said, "Good morning!" and shook hands with me. I went to his mother's room. She said, "Good morning. Bring me that bundle from my bureau and sit down here." I did as she told me. She placed the bundle [in] my hands and said, "Handle this and then put it in the top drawer of my bureau and lock it up." After I had done it she said, "Sit down. Do you remember that I told you about the Urim and Thummim when I told you about the Book of Mormon?" I answered "yes ma'am." She then told me I had just handled it. "You are not permitted to see it, but you have been permitted to handle it. You will live long after I am dead and gone and you can tell the Latter-day Saints, that you was permitted to handle the Urim and Thummim."

–Elizabeth J. D. Roundy, trans., Life History of Jane Elizabeth Manning James, Blacklds.org, http://www.blacklds.org/manning, accessed December 27, 2008.

Jane married Isaac James, after Joseph Smith's death.

Eudocia Baldwin Marsh, 1843-44

Eudocia Marsh, who grew up outside of Carthage, Illinois, visited Nauvoo on an outing with her family in late 1843 or 1844. Eudocia was about fifteen at the time. Her group dined at Smith's Mansion House. After dinner they examined the Egyptian mummies in an adjoining room. Eudocia provided an interesting description of Mother Lucy.

DURING THIS TIME of Mormon prosperity, while Nauvoo was growing rapidly and filling up with people from all parts of the world and becoming a place of considerable importance, many excursions and pleasure parties were gotten up to visit the City. Some of the members of our family joined such a party on one occasion, taking me with them.—We dined at the Mansion House, Smith's large Hotel. After dinner we were told that in an adjoining room some Egyptian Mummies were exhibited for a small sum.—Some of the party expressing a wish to see them, we went into the room where we found them presided over by the mother of the Prophet, a trim looking old lady in a black silk gown and white cap and kerchief.—With a long wand she pointed out to us the old King Pharaoh of the Exodus himself, with wife and daughter, and gave us a detailed account of their lives and doings three thousand years before.—Upon my asking her how she obtained all this information—she replied in a severely virtuous tone and a manner calculated to repress all doubt and further question—"My Son Joseph Smith has recently received a revelation from the Lord in regard to these people and times—and he has told all these things to me."—We left the house without faith in these revelations—neither did we believe in the old ladies [sic] faith in them which seemed hard on the mother of the "Prophet."

–Eudocia Baldwin Marsh, Archives, Knox College Library, Galesburg, Illinois; see also Douglas L. Wilson and Rodney O. Davis, eds., "Mormons in Hancock County: A Reminiscence," *Journal of the Illinois State Historical Society* 64 (Spring 1971): 36-38.

Mary Ann Hubbard, 1844

Mary Ann Hubbard and her husband, non-Mormon travelers, visited Nauvoo in June 1844, shortly before Joseph's death. The couple stayed a week at the Mansion house, dined with Joseph, and met Lucy while viewing the Egyptian relics. Mary Ann shared this experience with her family in a 1912 reminiscence.

WE JOURNEYED toward Nauvoo. . . . bad roads detained us at Nauvoo some days at the [Mansion House] hotel. . . . One afternoon [after lunch] it was raining very hard, and your uncle proposed that we should go down to the basement and see some mummies, the notice saying that one of them was that of Pharaoh's daughter. The exhibition was kept by Joe Smith's mother, who received us kindly and explained the history of the long dead laid out for inspection. I did not feel so solemn as one would have expected, for the old woman was all the time committing murder (of the King's English). The principal mummy had lost most of her fingers and toes, as they had been stolen for relics. I asked what had become of the gold plates which had the account of their inspired (?) writings. She replied, "O, they's took care of. You see they might have been stolen, and so they was give back to the one they got 'em of." When we had seen and heard enough, we prepared to go. We had bought a Mormon Bible and I had thanked Madam Smith for showing the relics, when your uncle unexpectedly inquired the charge, and paid the old lady for her polite attentions. I forget how much he paid, but I was sorry to have wasted my politeness in thanks.

As soon as we could leave, we went to Quincy; leaving our horses and carriage there, we took a steamer to Burlington, Iowa.

–Mary Ann Hubbard, *Family Memories* (Printed Privately, 1912).

Josiah Quincy, May 1844

Josiah Quincy III (1872-64). LOC.

Josiah Quincy, a mayor of Boston, Massachusetts and relative of President John Quincy Adams, visited Nauvoo, Illinois, in May 1844. Quincy's party spent a day with Joseph Smith, toured the Temple, met Lucy, and viewed the Egyptian scrolls and mummies in Mother Smith's possession.

66 **A**ND NOW COME with me," said the prophet, "and I will show you the curiosities." So say-

ing, he led the way to a lower room, where sat a venerable and respectable-looking lady. "This is my mother, gentlemen. The curiosities we shall see belong to her. They were purchased with her own money, at a cost of six thousand dollars;" and then, with deep feeling, were added the words, "And that woman was turned out upon the prairie in the dead of night by a mob." There were some pine presses fixed against the wall of the room. These receptacles Smith opened, and disclosed four human bodies, shrunken and black with age. "These are mummies," said the exhibitor. "I want you to look at that little runt of a fellow over there. He was a great man in his day. Why, that was Pharaoh Necho, King of Egypt!" Some parchments inscribed with hieroglyphics were then offered us. They were preserved under glass and handled with great respect. "That is the handwriting of Abraham, the Father of the Faithful," said the prophet. "This is the autograph of Moses, and these lines were written by his brother Aaron. Here we have the earliest account of the creation, from which Moses composed the first book of Genesis." The parchment last referred to showed a rude drawing of a man and woman, and a serpent walking upon a pair of legs. I ventured to doubt the propriety of providing the reptile in question with this unusual means of locomotion.

"Why, that's as plain as a pike-staff," was the rejoinder. "Before the Fall snakes always went about on legs, just like chickens. They were deprived of them, in punishment for their agency in the ruin of man." We were further assured that the prophet was the only mortal who could translate these mysterious writings, and that his power was given by direct inspiration.

It is well known that Joseph Smith was accustomed to make his revelations point to those sturdy business habits which lead to prosperity in this present life. He had little enough of that unmixed spiritual power which flashed out from the spare, neurasthenic body of Andrew Jackson. The prophet's hold upon you seemed to come from the balance and harmony of temperament which reposes upon a large physical basis. No association with the sacred phrases of scripture could keep the inspirations of this man from getting down upon the hard pan of practical affairs. "Verily I say unto you, let my servant, Sidney Gilbert, plant himself in this place and establish a store." So had run one of his revelations, in which no holier spirit than that of commerce is discernible. The exhibition of these August relics concluded with a similar descent into the hard modern world of fact. Monarchs, patriarchs, and parchments were very well in their way; but this was clearly the nineteenth century, when prophets must get a living and provide for their relations. "Gentlemen," said this bourgeois Mohammed, as he closed the cabinets, "those who see these curiosities generally pay my mother a quarter of a dollar."

The clouds had parted when we emerged from the chamber of curiosities, and there was time to see the temple before dinner.

–Josiah Quincy, *Figures of the Past from the Leaves of Old Journals*, 3rd ed. (Boston, 1883), 376-400.

Charles Francis Adams, 1844

Charles Adams, a member of Josiah Quincy's party, also reported this meeting with Lucy.

He [Joseph] then took us down into his mother's chamber and showed us four Egyptian mummies stripped and then undertook to explain the contents of a chart or manuscript which he said had been taken from the bosom of one of them. The cool impudence of this imposture amused me very much. "This," said he, "was written by the hand of Abraham and means so and so. If anyone denies it, let him prove the contrary. I say it." Of coarse [course], we were too polite to prove the negative, against a man fortified by revelation.

His mother looked on with attention and aided in the explanation whenever the prophet hesitated, from which I inferred that she was usually made the exponent of the writing to strangers. At the close, he notified us that for this instruction, his mother was in the habit of receiving a quarter of a dollar a piece which sum we paid forthwith.

–Henry Adams Jr., ed., "Charles Francis Adams Visits the Mormons in 1844," *Massachusetts Historical Society Proceedings* 68 (1952): 267-300.

Many others, like Church member Zina D. H. Jacobs, reported viewing the relics. Zina remembered seeing Lucy in August 1844.

I WENT WITH OLD Sister [blank] to see Mother Smith [and] the records.

–Maureen Ursenbach Beecher, ed., "'All Things Move in Order in the City:' The Nauvoo Diary of Zina Diantha Huntington Jacobs," *BYU Studies*, 19, no. 33 (Spring 1979): 285.

Edmund Flagg, 1844

Edmund Flagg's well-known travel account describes his meeting with Joseph Smith and an encounter with Lucy.

In an adjoining room, an Egyptian mummy, together with divers metallic plates covered with hieroglyphics, and connected by a ring, were exhibited by the prophet's mother, a very aged and infirm woman, who, poor old soul, with implicit faith, demonstrated their connexion [sic] with the revelations of her shameless son—at the charge of a quarter of a dollar a head.

–Edmund Flagg, "Nauvoo," in *The United States Illustrated; in Views of City and Country. With Descriptive and Historical Articles, Volume 2: The West; or, the States of the Mississippi Valley, and the Pacific*, edited by Charles A. Dana, (New York: Herrmann J. Meyer, 1855), 42-43.

Death of Joseph and Hyrum

Joseph and Hyrum Smith, profile portraits by Sutcliffe Maudsley, 1844. Joseph is holding a Bible and Hyrum the Doctrine and Covenants. Portraits courtesy L. Tom Perry Special Colletions, Harold B. Lee Library, Brigham Young University, Provo, Utah.

David Kilbourne

Joseph and Hyrum Smith were killed at Carthage Jail, Carthage, Illinois, on June 27, 1844. David Kilbourne, a land speculator and railroad builder, witnessed some of the day's events. David wrote to Reverend T. Dent, Lancashire, England, June 29, 1844. Kilbourne's account of Joseph's and Hyrum's deaths, published in the *London Record,* was the first to reach England. Kilbourne described the scene at the Mansion House soon after word reached Nauvoo of events in Carthage.

THE MORMON Prophet Joe Smith & his brother Hyrum are no more. I have just returned from Nauvoo & I this day looked upon the lifeless remains of these two men—the great heads & leaders of Mormonism.

[On the 27th] I put up at Joes tavern. . . . About 4 O'Clock the next morning Friday June 28th . . . [a] messenger arrived at Joes tavern. . . [with the news]. I immediately dressed & went down, saw Joes wife & children about the house, but saw no manifestations of grief on the part of any one save Joes mother who made her appearance at the door in the course of the morning & enquired who had killed her sons.

–David Kilbourne, Letter to Reverend T. Dent, Lancashire, England, June 29, 1844, David Wells Kilbourne (1803-1876), Kilbourne Collection, Iowa State Archives, Des Moines, Iowa; cited in Warren Jennings, "The Work of Death Has Commenced: "The Lynching of an American Prophet," Draft manuscript, Warren A. Jennings Papers, P109, f40, CofC Archives.

Carthage Jail.

James Linforth

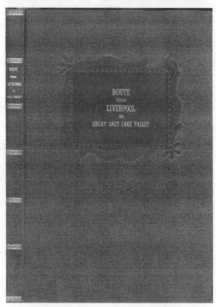

ROUTE FROM LIVERPOOL
TO
Great Salt Lake Valley
ILLUSTRATED

James Linforth's epic Mormon volume, *Route from Liverpool to Great Salt Lake Valley*, narrates the pivotal moment in Lucy's life:

L UCY TOOK UP HER residence with her son Joseph, and was shortly afterwards taken very sick, and brought nigh to death. She had scarcely recovered when she was called to suffer almost over-whelming grief for the assassination of her sons Joseph

JOSEPH SMITH.

and Hyrum. When she was permitted to see the corpses of her murdered sons, her sorrow was great indeed. "I was," she says, "swallowed up in the depths of my afflictions; and though my soul was filled with horror past imagination, yet, I was dumb, until I arose again to contemplate the spectacle before me. Oh! At that moment how my mind

HYRUM SMITH.

flew through every scene of sorrow and distress which we had passed together, in which they had shown the innocence and sympathy which filled their guileless hearts. As I looked upon their peaceful, smiling countenances, I seemed almost to hear them say— 'Mother, weep not for us, we have overcome the world by love; we carried to them the Gospel, that their souls might be saved; they slew us for our testimony, and thus placed us beyond their power; their ascendancy is for a moment, ours is an eternal triumph.'"

–James Linforth, *Route from Liverpool to Great Salt Lake Valley* (Liverpool, England: F. D. Richards, 1855), 71.

Lucy reportedly positioned herself between her dead sons, rested a hand on each body, [and] cried out, "My God, my God, why hast thou forsaken this family!"
–Anderson, *Lucy's Book*, 749.

Family friend Sarah M. Kimball recalled Lucy could not be consoled. Eventually, the grieving woman said, "How could they kill my boys! O how could they kill them when they were so *precious*! I am sure they would not harm anybody in the world."
–Sarah M. Kimball, Letter to

Serepta Heywood, n. d. , Kimball Papers, LDS Church Library; cited in Richard Holzapfel and Jeni Holzapfel, *Women of Nauvoo* (Salt Lake City: Bookcraft, 1992), 130.

After the funeral of Joseph Jr. and Hyrum Smith, while still living with Emma Lucy began publically sharing her opinion about property ownership and succession issues. Willard Richards recalled:

JULY 2, 1844. Tuesday. A.M. went to see Emma. She is in trouble because Mother Smith is making disturbance about the property in Josephs hands. Mother Smith wants Samuel to move into Nauvoo and take the Patriarchs office and says the church ought to support him. There is considerable danger if the family begins to dispute about the property that Joseph's creditors will come forward and use up all the property there is. If they will keep still there is property enough to pay the debts and plenty left for other uses. I had much talk with Emma on the subject.

–George D. Smith, *An Intimate Chronicle: The Journals of Williams Clayton* (Salt Lake City, Utah: Signature Books), 136

Succession

"**N**o explicit outline of presidential succession [was] in print [when Joseph died].... Between 1834 and 1844, Joseph Smith had by word or action established precedents or authority for eight possible methods of succession."

–D. Michael Quinn, "The Mormon Succession Crisis of 1844," *BYU Studies* 16, no. 2 (Winter 1976): 187.

Despite the wishes of Mother Smith, Emma, and some others, the Quorum of Twelve slowly but surely strengthened their control of the leadership of the Church.

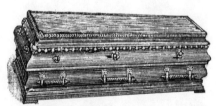

Sadly, while still reeling from the deaths of Joseph and Hyrum, Lucy lost another son. Samuel H. (1808-1844) mysteriously became ill and died in July, only a month after the events in Carthage.

Wilford Woodruff, 1844

Wilford Woodruff recorded an August 1844 visit with Lucy in his journal:

23D (I MET) WITH the quorum of the Twelve in council or some of them. I visited Emma Smith the widow of the prophet. She let me have a peace of oak for a Staff—out of the Coffin—of the Prophet Joseph who was inhumanly martered in Carthage Ill in company with his brother Hiram [Hyrum]. Emma also let me have a Pair of gloves composed of white cotton and Mrs Woodruff a cotton handkerchief both of which the Prophet wore while living.

We called upon Sister Mary Smith widow of Hiram Smith the Patriarch. She gave us some hair from the head of Joseph Smith, Hiram Smith, Samuel Smith, & Don Carloss Smith, all brothers of the same Parents. I also obtained some hair of the quorum of the Twelve Apostles in the Church of Jesus Christ of the Latter Day Saints. My object was in putting a portion of each in the top of my staff as a

Cane with Joseph's hair in handle, photograph by Val Brinkerhoff, courtesy
International Society Daughters of Utah Pioneers.

relick of those noble men, master spirits of the nineteenth century, to hand down to my posterity, to deposit in the most Holy and Sacred place in the Holy temple of GOD, on the consecrated Hill of Zion.

I next visited Mother Lucy Smith, the mother of those noble men even the Lords anointed, whose names were Joseph, Hiram, Samuel and Don Carloss, and the wife of Joseph Smith sen. the first Patriarch of the last dispensation. All those men fell directly or indirectly as marters for the cause of truth and of God, Joseph and Hiram being shot in Cold Blood.

The Old Mother and Prophetess felt most heart broaken at the loss of her Children and the wicked and Cruel treatment she had received from the hands of the gentile world. She begged a blessing at my hands. I lade my hands upon her head and proclaimed the following by the Spirit of God.

The following blessing was proclaimed upon the head of Mother Lucy Smith (the Mother of the Prophet seer and Revelator Joseph and his brethren) on the 23d day of August 1844 under the hands of Elder Wilford Woodruff of the quorum of the Twelve:

Lucy's blessing.

Mother Smith's Blessing

Wilford Woodruff.

BELOVED MOTHER IN Israel according to your request I lay my hands upon your head, in the name of Jesus Christ of Nazareth and by virtue of the Holy Priesthood and the [keys] of the kingdom of God to bestow a blessing upon you for thou art worthy of all blessings.

As I lade my hands upon thy husband Joseph Smith sen. the Patriarch of the Church by his request to bless him as he lay upon his bed like Jacob of old ready to gather up his feet and sleep with his fathers, and I about to take my departure over the sea to visit foreign nations, which was the last time we ever met on earth in like manner do I esteem it a blessing and a privilege to lay my hands upon your head, in your decline of life to leave with you my parting blessing as I am again Called to bid farewell to my native Country and visit foreign Climes to bear record of the word of God.

We may never meet again on earth. But I thank my God that I have this privilege of blessing thee, for my heart is full of blessings for thee for thou art the greatest Mother in Israel. The sons thou hast bourn and Cherished are the most noble spirits that ever graced humanity or tabernacled in flesh. Their work shall be had in honorable remembrance through all generations of men. Though counted among transgressors, they like the Messiah have shed their blood for the sins of the people, and freely offered their lives and sealed their testimony.

Thou hast lived and stood to see the fall of thy sons by the rage of gentile hands. And like an impenatrible rock in the midst of the mighty deep thou hast remained unmoved untill God has given thee [the] desires of thy heart in seeing the keys of the Kingdom of God held in the hands of thy Posterity so planted in the earth that they shall never be taken from it untill he reigns whose right it is to reign.

Let thy heart be Comforted in the midst of thy sorrow, for thou shalt be had in honorable rememberance forever in the Congregations of the righteous. Thou shalt be remembered in thy wants during the remainder of thy day. And when thou art called to depart thou canst lie down in peace having seen the salvation of God, in laying an everlasting foundation for the deliverance <of Israel> through the instrumentality of thy sons.

I seal upon your head all the blessings of the fullness of the gospel and of the Church of the first born, and all those blessings that have been sealed upon you heretofore. If we meet no more on earth we will meet in the morn of the first resurrection whare you shall receive thrones, powers, a dominion and kingdom, in Connexion with thy husband in his high exhaltation in the linage of his fathers. I seal all these blessings upon your head in the name of Jesus Christ and by virtue of the Holy Priesthood, Amen.

—*Woodruff's Journal*, August 23, 1844, 2: 450-452.

Jonathan Wright Letter

While her son William B. Smith was away performing a mission in the eastern United States, Lucy asked Jonathan C. Wright to draft a letter for her.

August 28, 1844

DEAR BROTHER Smith:

I have this morning called to see your mother whom I found as well as could be expected, and at her request have agreed to write this letter, although measurably a stranger to you in one sense of the word; but claiming you as a brother in the church, as a servant of the Most High God—I feel quite at liberty, by the request of your mother, to introduce myself in this manner to your better acquaintance. At present things in general wear in some degree the appearance of peace in the city and county, although from Warsaw and Carthage there are almost constant ebullitions and slanderous eruptions, as usual, belching forth from the infernal subterraneous vault of Mount Sharp's Crater, which is spreading and ejecting its poisonous venom more or less through every neighborhood in the county, and not alone in the county, but among all the opposers of truth throughout all the territory of its circulation. Matters in the city are truly encouraging to the saints. The Twelve are with us in the power of Israel's God—demonstrating to us every Sabbath with great power the organization of the kingdom; I believe entirely in the satisfaction of every faithful Latter Day Saint. Although there has been much said about who should take Joseph's place as our leader or guardian since the death of the Prophet—but on last Sunday it was told us, that last winter the Twelve were called, ordained, anointed and qualified, and were fully vested with authority and power from on high to meet just such an emergency and to bear off the kingdom of God triumphantly to the nations of the earth, in spite of earth or hell, devils or mobbers—while all the saints unitedly, with loud voices say, amen and so it will be.

As for the news of the city, temporally; I have only to say to you, that it is much healthier here than former seasons have been, as I have been informed by the oldest citizens. The principle disease of which we complain is Diarrhea, and that is mostly confined to children. The Temple is going up, I will say, rapidly.—The present calculation is, to continue on the walls (hot or cold) until they are completed; a number of carpenters are also engaged in doing some inside work, and there is a great general zeal manifested in trying to forward the building in every particular as fast as possible, and as Brother Cahoon remarked the other day upon the stand, "that he had only to say the word, and the fur flew." I write you these little items, because I believe you will be glad to read them.

Sister Emma is going to leave the Mansion this week, and move into her old house where Dr. Richards lives. Elder Marks will occupy the Mansion. Mother Smith is going to live with her son in law, Arthur. He has been quite sick but has principally recovered. Brother Hyrum's family are well. Elder Taylor has so far recovered that he is able to ride in his carriage and attend meetings. Emigration is coming in slowly but increasing.

I know of nothing further to write to you except your affectionate mother's prayers and blessings—she prays that God will remember you, and sustain and support you under all circumstances, keep you humble and faithful, even unto the end; and that God will bless you and provide for you—that you will shortly be able to come and once more on this side of the vail, comfort with your presence, the heart of her who has borne you into the world, and who has often at midnight hours, from your infant hours until the present date, sent up prayers mingled with tears to the God whose omnipotent power governs heaven and earth—even unto him does she continue to pray, for your health, prosperity, and finally, your eternal salvation.

She has heard nothing from you since Bro. Kimball returned. She has heard your wife is dead. I will say that not only your mother would like to hear from you, but many others of your brethren and sisters in Nauvoo, would also be pleased to hear from you—as well as your unworthy friend who now writes to you. I would therefore say in behalf of your mother, write, and write soon.

Yours in the new and everlasting covenant

Jonathan C. Wright

P. S. Your mother wishes me to say something about the death of your brother Samuel; the reason I did not embrace an account of his death in the above is, I supposed that you had learned all the particulars in relation to his death, but she fears you have not. Samuel died in consequence of being chased by the mob for 2 hours on the prairie at full speed, and being very hot weather, he was overcome by fatigue.—he died shortly after [he] moved to Nauvoo, where he was taken with the Fever, and died after about ten day's confinement—His remains were interred near the same place with Joseph and Hyrum. Give yourself no uneasiness about your mother—the Twelve say she shant want. J. C. W.

–Jonathan C. Wright, Letter to William Smith, August 28, 1844, Nauvoo, Illinois, *The Prophet* 1, no. 31 (December 21, 1844): 2; Typescript, P96, f75, CofC Archives.

BIOGRAPHICAL SKETCHES

OF

JOSEPH SMITH,

THE

PROPHET,

AND HIS

Progenitors for many Generations.

BY

LUCY SMITH,

MOTHER OF THE PROPHET.

Liverpool:
PUBLISHED FOR ORSON PRATT BY S. W. RICHARDS,
15, WILTON STREET.
London:
SOLD AT THE LATTER-DAY SAINTS' BOOK DEPOT,
35, JEWIN STREET;
AND BY ALL BOOKSELLERS.
1853.

Title page of Lucy's history.

Lucy Writes Her History

After the death of her sons, Lucy began dictating her life history with the help of Martha Coray, a Nauvoo school teacher with a reputation for transcribing many of Joseph Smith's sermons. Lucy advised her son William of her intentions via letter:

MY MOST affectionate and only remaining Son, I have just received your letter bearing date Dec. 23 I rejoiced to hear from you once more Although we are both of us in deep affliction. Do not think that your Mother or your Sisters are indifferent to your present distress. We look to you as the sole remaining male Suport [sic] of your Fathers house William I once had 5 noble and manly sons A compa[n]ion who was the delight of my heart besides 3 dutiful affectionate Daughters whose affections with the favor of God made me as happy as it was possible for a mother woman to be. 4 of those sons with their Father are laid in the cold and silent mansion of the tomb By what By Whom am I deprived of my children and made a Widow my health destroyed and my peace of mind blasted for ever on Earth Angels Patriotic men and God declare that it was by malicious persecution & the dagger of the dark assassin where is my last remaining son the solace of my age Ah he is a pilgrim in a strange land traversing the Earth [to] preach salvation to those who if they do not rize up as advocates of equal and consitutional rights will hold up their hands to Heaven in the day of judgment dyed like crimson with your brothers blood But William I believe that your skirts are clear of the blood of this generation 14 years you have warned them faithfully.

The nation with whom you have labored have like Jeshurim [Jerusalem?] waxed fat and kicked against the truth Having risen up in wrath and Shed the blood of the righteous but let it pass they will one day stand before God face to face with the stain for the truths sake to give account for the deeds done in the body.

I received your letter addressed to Bro. Phelps through the colum[n]s of the prophet first by the Hand of bro Heber Kimball as afterwards it was brought to me by Bro. Phelps himself & who answered it immediately according to your request Bro Heber Kimball was highly delighted with it said it pleased him the best of anything he had seen in a long time The 12 are very anxious to see you and the church are all waiting to receive you with open arms They are continually enquiring after poor Carolines health and have a great

desire to see her once more they weep over her afflictions and pray for her recovery My Dear Daughter Caroline do not immagine [sic] your Mother forgets you My prayers and suplications are poured out by night and by day for you and I do hope that God will in mercy Spare you to come back to Nauvoo that we may behold your face again in the flesh and may God grant that you may live to be [a] comfort to your Husband and to us as also be able to raise your dear children that I love as my own for they are mine and I love them as such Kiss them for me and tell them Grand Mother longs to see them Trust in God my Dear child and try to live so that we may meet again your sisters pray for you and they wish me to give their love to you and say that they remmember you always in their prayers—

William I have something to communicate with regard to business I have by the councill of the 12 undertaken a history of the family that is my Fathers Family and my own now I want you to endeavor to raise by subscription for the work enough means to obtain paper for printing it Will the Saints abroad have the kindness to assist me in this thing that I may be able to accomplish this work before I follow your Father and Brothers to that bourne from whence no traveler returns I

Martha Coray, Lucy's scribe.

suppose if I were with the Saints they would be glad to hear me relate those things which I design committing to paper The Brethren here are very anxious about the matter and would help me if they could but they are poor and if those abroad will do as much as those at home in proportion to their means it would soon be done I shall need at least $100 dollars worth of paper.

The friends are all well Emma is in health and her babe is healthy grows finely Agness is here with her children She Sends her love to you both and your children Mary and Sister Thomson wish to be remembered in love also Sop[hr]onia and Lovina send an affectionate remembrance of you all we have just received a letter from Catharine She is well they live in Beardstown But they want to move to Nauvoo I live with Arthur and Lucy who are very kind and send their love to you and Caroline and the children

There was a mistake in the printer with regard to Alvin's age when he died The paper states that he was nearly 32 this is wrong his age was between 24 & 25 If the brethren would sign a subscription for the book which I design publishing and pay half the worth of it in money into your hands in order that you might be able to buy a small quantity of paper and bring with you it would assist me in my present necessity very much and I should be extremely grateful to them for the favor I think it would be an assistance to you and myself too People are often enquiring of me the particulars of Joseph's getting the plates seeing the angels at first and many other thing[s] which Joseph never wrote or published I have told many things pertaining to these matters to different persons to gratify their curiosity indeed have almost destroyed my lungs giving these recitals to those who felt anxious to hear them I have now concluded to write down every particular as far as possible and if those who wish to read them will help me a little they can have it all in one place to read at their leasure—I have now used up my sheet and must bid you adieu for the present I am as ever your affectionate Mother

Lucy Smith

My son I intend if I accomplish the book I have commenced that it shall be an assistance to you and your sisters and believe it will be a benefit to you all. Lucy's babe Don Carlos Smith is a bright playful boy and just begins to run alone.

–Lucy Mack Smith, Letter to William Smith, January 23, 1845, Nauvoo, holograph, LDS Church Library. Cited in Kyle R. Walker, "Katharine Smith Salisbury's Recollections of Joseph's Meetings with Moroni," *BYU Studies* 41, no. 3 (2002): fn. 2, p. 5.

Martha's husband, Howard Coray, recalled,

I N THE FALL OF 1844, I procured the music hall for a schoolroom. It was large enough to accommodate 150 students and I succeeded in filling the room, or nearly so. In running the school I had my wife's assistance, and also Brother John M. Woolley's. Sometime in the winter following, Mother Smith came to see my wife

about getting her to write the history of Joseph, to act in the matter only as her, Mother Smith's, amanuensis. This my wife was persuaded to do and so dropped the school. Not long had she worked in this direction before I was requested also to drop the school and turn it over to Brother William and Woolley and help her in the matter of the history. After consulting President Young, who advised me to do so, I consented and immediately set to with my might. We labored together until the work was accomplished, which took us until nearly the close of 1845.

–Diary of Howard Coray, Copy of holograph, MS 2034, LDS Church Library.

Howard and Martha Coray home

COPYRIGHT

Lucy applied for and obtained the copyright for her history. The copyright, granted July 18, 1845, affirms the work to be: "The History of Lucy Smith . . . an account of the many persecutions, trials and afflictions which I and my family have endured in bringing forth the Book of Mormon, and establishing the Church of Jesus Christ of Latter Day Saints."

–Copyright Records, Illinois, Vol. 18 [1821-48], July 18, 1845, Library of Congress, Washington, D.C.); cited in Marquardt & Walters, *Inventing Mormonism*, 221.

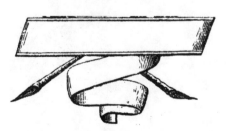

To the right: Lucy Mack Smith's bonnett, photograph by Val Brinkerhoff.

Lucy lived near Joseph and Emma during most of their seventeen years of marriage. Lucy had come to admire Emma after seeing her daughter-in-law respond well to a variety of difficult situations. While dictating her history to Martha Corey, Lucy paid special tribute to Emma:

I HAVE NEVER SEEN A woman in my life, who would endure every species of fatigue and hardship, from month to month, and from year to year, with that unflinching courage, zeal, and patience, which she has ever done; for I know that which she has had to endure—she has been tossed upon the ocean of uncertainty—she has breasted the storms of persecution, and buffeted the rage of men and devils, which would have borne down almost any other women.

–*Lucy Mack Smith History* (Liverpool, 1853), 169.

Hosea Stout, February 1845

Hosea Stout, profile by Sutcliffe Maudsley, ca. 1842, courtesy Church Archives, The Church of Jesus Christ of Latter-day Saints.

Hosea Stout wrote,

23RD SUNDAY [February 1845]. In the forenoon went with my wife to a meeting at Bishop Hales Elder Dunham preached. Sister Smith the mother of Joseph the Prophet and Seer was there. She spoke to the congregation and told her feelings and the trials and troubles she had passed through in establishing the Church of Christ and the persecutions & afflictions which her sons & husband had passed through and the cruel and unheard of martyrdom of Joseph & Hyrum

which had took place so lately, and exhorted the brethren & sisters to be faithful and bring up their children in the way they should go and not have them running about in the streets as was too much allowed now.

All were deeply affected with the remarks of this "Mother," of the "mothers in Israel" for she spoke with the most feeling and heart broken manner of the troubles she had passed through.

– Juanita Brooks, ed., *On the Mormon Frontier: The Diary of Hosea Stout, 1844-1861*, February 23, 1845 (Salt Lake City, UT: University of Utah Press, 1964), 22.

Engraving of Lucy Mack Smith from *William Smith on Mormonism*.

Lucy *and* William B. Smith

Following his brothers' deaths, William Smith returned to Nauvoo on May 4, 1845, urging the Twelve to make him Patriarch of the Church. The Twelve acquiesced and he was ordained May 25, 1845.

–Linda Newell and Valeen Avery, *Mormon Enigma: Emma Hale Smith* (Urbana, IL: University of Illinois Press, 1994), 215.

William explained his actions in 1845, including the loss and burial of his wife Caroline.

When I cam[e] home I went to Emma's and stayed there some time, where I and mine were kindly and affectionately treated, and Caroline received every attention that the strongest love and affection could dictate. She was interred with the usual ceremonies in the vault prepared for the Smith family near the Temple. But in a short time after, it being very warm weather, her body was taken from the vault and placed in the graveyard, by request of the hands working on the temple. But I am now preparing a place in Emma's garden to bury her, and I am getting some grave stones made and fence to ornament her grave.

Soon after her death, I moved into the house formerly occupied by Wm. Marks, as I found it would be necessary for me to keep house; and to avoid the censure and jealousy of some good brethren and sisters, if I hired women to take charge of my household affairs, and kept them about me, and as my little girls were running wild, and my clothes needed some attention, I have broken through sectarian tradition, and in the course of about a month taken another wife. . . . My little girls are well and send their love to you. Geo. and Betsey are enjoying good health. Mother Smith is rather unwell this summer.—But most of your relations with whose circumstances I am acquainted with are generally in good health.   Wm. Smith

–William Smith, Letter to Joshua Grant, Jr., August 12, 1845, Nauvoo, Illinois, *Nauvoo Neighbor*, 3, no. 16 (August 20, 1845): 485.

Nauvoo Neighbor masthead, courtesy Larry Faria.

Lucy's Dreams

Engraving of William B. Smith, from *William Smith on Mormonism.*

In June 1845, Lucy dreamed that William was to be the President of the Church. Rumors of Lucy's "vision" prompted an attempt by the Twelve "to placate the Smiths and win their support."

—Mormon Enigma, 216, 217.

Apostle John Taylor's wife told him about Lucy's vision. Taylor noted in his journal:

Friday, June 27th, 1845. This was the anniversary of the day that Brothers Joseph and Hyrum were killed and myself shot. . . . In the evening Mrs. Taylor showed me a copy of a vision that Mother Lucy Smith had, stating that her son William was head over the Church; the following is a copy:

Brothers and Children, I was much troubled and felt as if I had the sins of whole world to bear, and the burthen of the Church; and I felt that there something wrong. I called on the Lord to show me what was wrong, and if it was me. I called upon him until I slept. I then heard a voice calling on me saying awake, awake, awake, for thy only son that thou hast living, they for his life have laid a snare. My aged servant Joseph who was the first patriarch of this Church, and my servant Hyrum who was the second patriarch, my servant Joseph who was Prophet and Seer, and my servants Samuel, William, and Don Carlos they were the first founders, fathers, and heads of this Church, raised up in these last days, and thou art the mother, and thy daughters have helped, and they are the daughters in Israel, and have helped raise up this Church. Arise, Arise, Arise, and take thy place you know not what has been in the hearts of some; but he said thou shalt know. He told me what it was; but I shall not tell. (I saw William in a room full of armed men and he having no weapons. They have crushed him down, if it had not been for the power of God; and many of the family would have been cut off, the Lord having softened their hearts. Two amongst them had blacker hearts than the rest, and I know who were, and I will tell them if they will come to me. Brigham Young and Kimball know it is so, and dare not deny it.) Call upon the Twelve, let things be set in order, and keep their hearts pure from this time henceforth, the voice saith be merciful, and then Zion shall arise and flourish as a rose. What I was told I cannot tell. Thou art the mother in Israel, and tell thy children all to walk uprightly. Thy son William he shall have power over the Churches, he is father in Israel over the patriarchs and the whole of the Church, he is the last of the lineage that is raised up in these last days. He is patriarch to regulate the affairs of the Church. He is President over all the Church, they can not take his apostleship away from him. The Presidency of the Church belongs to William, he being the last of the heads of the Church, according to the lineage, he having inherited it from the family from before the foundation of the world. Thou art a mother in Israel. Thy spirit arose and said in eternity, that it would take a body to be a mother to [the] Prophet who should be raised up to save the last dispensation. And, the spirit said unto me be faithful (and that I had been faithful.) And tell the Church to be faithful. And the spirit said I should live until I was satisfied with life.

Brothers and Children, I want you to take notice the burthen of the Church [rests on William.]

2nd Vision. Joseph came to me and said "that day is coming when I shall wave the scepter [sic] of power over my enemies. Be patient my brothers and sisters, the day is coming when you shall have eternal life and be rewarded for all your troubles."

3rd Vision. Father came to me and I said Father have you come. And he said "Yes." I said tell me where you have been? And he said "I have been all around here. I have come to you again to tell you one thing certain, which I have told you many times before. It is my prayers and the prayers of our sons that you live to take care of William and my daughters, and see that they have their rights and standing where they ought to have it. He turned to go away, and I said I will go with you. He said you must stay.

The following persons were present at the time this vision was related:

William Smith,
A. Milliken,
W. J. Salisbury,

David Elliott,
Robt. Campbell,
Elias Smith,
Joseph Cain,
Bro. Stringham,
Chas. Kelly,
Bro. McLery,
Mrs. Taylor,
Mrs. Milliken,
Mrs. Salisbury,
Mrs. McLery,
Mrs. Kelly,
Mrs. Sherman.

–Dean C. Jessee, ed., "The John Taylor Nauvoo Journal: January 1845-September 1845," *BYU Studies*, 23, no. 3 (Summer 1983): 63-64.

The Twelve arranged a meeting with Lucy and William. But William elected not to attend, prompting the following letter from Brigham Young.

D[EA]R BRO. WILLIAM:
A majority of the quorum of the twelve, Bishops Whitney and Miller, and brother Cahoon one of the Temple committee have met to hold a little conversation with Mother Smith at her house. We expected to have had your company but were disappointed. We however have received a note from you which we feel to answer before we separate so that it may be sanctioned or rejected by Mother Smith. We have had considerable talk with Mother Smith, and find her possessing the best of feelings towards the whole church.

As to your requests in your letter [having the right to administer all ordinances in the world and no one standing at your head] we would say we are perfectly willing, and wish to have all things right, but there are some ordinances in the church that cannot be administered by any person out of this place at present. ... But as to your right to officiate in the office of Patriarch, we say you have the right to officiate in all the world, wherever your lot may be cast and no one to dictate or control you excepting the twelve, which body of men must preside over the whole Church in all the world.

We hope and trust there will be no feelings. Say nothing about matters and things. If you want peace so do we, and let us talk together in peace, and help to build up the kingdom. If this does not meet with your feelings brother William write me again, or come and see me, and we will make all things right for we surely want peace and the salvation of the people. We remain as ever your brethren and wellwishers.

Brigham Young

P. S. We have read this to Mother

Smith, Catherine, Lucy and Arthur and they express their satisfaction with it as well as those of the council who are present. B.Y.

–Brigham Young, Letter to William Smith, June 30, 1845, Nauvoo, Illinois, LDS Church Library; P96, f76, CofC Archives.

In July 1845, following this meeting, Bishops Whitney and Miller sponsored a dinner in honor of the Smith family that included seven widows [Mother Smith, Emma, Mary, Levira, Agnes, Mercy Thompson, and perhaps the widow of the martyrs' uncle]. "The Twelve waited on the tables, serving the family members both food and kindness."

–*Mormon Enigma*, 217, fn. 31; See also B. H. Roberts, *Comprehensive History of the Church*, 7: 433.

John Taylor noted,

Wednesday, July 9th, 1845. [In the afternoon I attended] a party with Mrs. Taylor, where the Smith family wew invited, the Twelve, and the Temple Committee. Mother Smith, William and all the connections of the Smith family, between one hundred and one hundred and fifty were present.

–Dean C. Jessee, ed., "The John Taylor Nauvoo Journal," *BYU Studies* 23, no. 3 (Summer 1983): 77.

But William believed his ordination as Patriarch surpassed every other priesthood office and wished to be appointed as caretaker president of the church until young Joseph III was old enough to take his father's place.

John D. Lee

John D. Lee.

Church member John D. Lee recalled,

I HEARD MOTHER Smith, the mother of Joseph the Prophet, plead with Brigham Young, with tears, not to rob young Joseph of his birthright, which his father, the Prophet, bestowed upon him previous to his death. That young Joseph was to succeed his father as the leader of the Church, and it was his right in the line of the priesthood. "I know it," replied Brigham, "don't worry or take any trouble, Mother Smith; by so doing you are only laying the knife to the throat of the child. If it is known that he is the rightful successor of his father, the enemy of the Priesthood will seek his life. He is too young to lead this people now, but when he arrives at mature age he shall have his place. No one shall rob him of it." This conversation took place in the Masonic Hall at Nauvoo, in 1846. Several persons were then present.

–John D. Lee, *Mormonism Unveiled: Or the Life and Confessions of the Late Mormon Bishop John D. Lee* (St. Louis, MO: Bryan, Brand & Company, 1877), 161.

During the summer of 1845, while politicking for William's position, Lucy recalled a blessing given by her husband to young Joseph III at Kirtland, Ohio.

Lucy dictated Joseph III's blessing to Martha Corey from memory.

Blessing of Joseph Smith the Son of Joseph who was the son of Joseph Smith the 1st given in Kirtland by his Grandfather when he was yet a very small child.

"I LAY MY HANDS upon your head to bless you Your name is after the name of your father You are Joseph the third You shall live long upon the Earth And after you are grown up you shall have wisdom knowledge and understanding And shall search into the mysteries of the kingdom of God Your heart shall be open to all men And your hand shall be open to relieve the wants of the poor You shall be admired by all who shall behold you You shall be an honor to your Father and Mother And a comfort to your Mother You shall be a help to your brothers and you shall have power to carry out all that your Father shall leave undone When you become of age And you shall have power to wield the sword of Laban."

The within is the gleanings of the blessings of Joseph Smith the surviving heir of the Prophet and

Seer as much as could be obtained from his Grandmother when in the midst of the Gentiles at a time when to write such things endangered the boys life what follows is not the prerogative of the writer to say— suf[f]ice it [to] say there is a clue to all these things in the covenants of his Fathers priesthood which he committed to man while yet alive

writ[t]en by Lucy Smith amanuensis Clerk

N.B. This must not be copied except by order of the Authorities of the church or the owner as it was forbidden by the one who gave it
given by Mother Smith from memory Summer of 1845
Blessing of Joseph Smith 3rd

–Lucy Mack Smith, 1845
Statement of Blessing of Joseph
Smith III given by Joseph Smith,
Sr., Kirtland, Ohio, Smith Papers,
P70-1, f15, CofC Archives.

John Taylor

John Taylor visited Lucy again in June 1845.

Tuesday, June 17th, 1845.
WENT TO MOTHER Lucy Smith's, by her request to read some of her

John Taylor, ca. 1850.

history, to see if it was fit or ready for publication. I had an interesting conversation with the old lady; wherein she related many things concerning the family that pleased as well as instructed me; though now quite an aged woman, the power of her memory is surprising, she is able to relate circumstances connected with the family, with great distinctness and accuracy; she is an honor as well as an ornament to the family [to which] she belongs.

–"The John Taylor Nauvoo
Journal, *BYU Studies*, 23 (Summer
1983): 52.

Later that month the Twelve proposed to lease the Mansion House for three to five years and approached Emma to negotiate acceptable terms for managing the property. Willard Richards reported that Emma vacillated about a decision, saying she might stay in Nauvoo and run the Mansion or might lease it out and move to Quincy. In the end, on August 2 Emma sold two blocks of land to Church trustees for five hundred fifty dollars and entered into a lease allowing use of the Nauvoo Mansion House.

–Journal History, January 18, 1846, LDS Church Library.

Joseph Heywood, Almon Babbitt, and Amos Fullmer were elected as trustees of the estate of Joseph Smith Jr. on January 4, replacing Newel K. Whitney and George Miller.

Certificate of George Miller & N. K. Whitney of the election of Almon W. Babbitt Joseph L. Heywood & John S. Ful[l]mer as trustees. Jany 4, 1846.
N. K. Whitney
Swears to this before Isaac Higbee J. P.
Right: Drawing of Mansion House by Campbell, courtesy LDS Archives.

–Certificate of George Miller, January 4, 1844, Hancock County Mortgage Record, No. 2, page 144, Holograph, History of Hancock County, Documents, Petitions, and Excerpts, 1841-1905, CofC Archives, P11-4, f1.

Lucy felt welcome in Emma's home but was independent by nature. Feeble as she was, she still desired a home of her own.

–Newell and Avery, Mormon Enigma, 353, fn. 32.

[The Twelve] invited Lucy Smith to inspect the property they had recently purchased from Emma. They offered to let her choose one block for herself and daughters. After careful inspection Lucy made her choice and requested that "the Church build her a house like Brother Kimball's" fine one.

–Joseph L. Heywood, unpublished Heywood family history; in Mormon Enigma, 217.

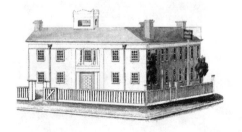

Wilford Woodruff

Wilford Woodruff, courtesy Church Archives, The Church of Jesus Christ of Latter-day Saints.

A difference centering upon a carriage for Lucy was representative of a growing gulf between the Smith family and church administrators. Wilford Woodruff recorded Brigham Young's perspective of the matter:

WHEN I WAS IN Nauvoo I Commenced to build me a Carriage. William [Smith] got up a rumor that I was Finishing a Carriage for my own use which Joseph had Comenced for his mother. Then Mother Smith soon reported that I was building her a Carriage and the first time she got me in company she asked me for that Carriage. I did not care much about the carriage but I was sorry to have her take that Course.... Mother Smith was under the influence of Wm Smith and the spirit of Aposticy [sic] which was in Nauvoo.

— Woodruff's Journal, February 13, 1859, 5: 289.

Brigham Young

Brigham Young wrote to Lucy promising to provide support and trying to minimize the damage.

Brigham Young, by Piercy in the 1850s.

MY DEAR AGED mother Smith, for so I feele to caul you, my mother in the gospel, and the mother of my Dear Brother Joseph, the prophet and se-ere.

I feele to wright to you as I can-not come to see you this morning. I lern that you have feelings, that is not plesent concerning the caredge that I have succeeded in geting built on the tithing, the caredge is not yet done, when it is you shall relize all that you have had promised to you by me or the trustees. I beg of you not to have enny unplesent feelings on the subject, it is nothing but a comon caredge that is perishable and will soon be decayed, and so shall our earthly tabernacles, and I pray the all mighty God our Heven-ly Father to help us, to so live and walk before him that we may be ex-cepted of him. All that I have is at your command to make you happy the little time you have to live with us. I shall caul and see you as soon as I can convenently. May the Lord Bles you and comfort your hart. I am your son and friend as ever.

–Brigham Young, Letter to Lucy Smith, August 2, 1845, LDS Church Library; Quoted in Dean C. Jessee, "The Writings of Brigham Young," *The Western Historical Quarterly* 4, no. 3 (July, 1973): 286.

Lucy's Support

LUCY MACK SMITH publicly endorsed the lead-ership of the Twelve over the Church at the conference of October 7, 1845. And as one of the members of the Holy Order, she also joined with Brigham Young and the apostles in the endowment ceremonies of the Nauvoo Temple in December 1845.

–William Clayton Journal, De-cember 10, 1845; Heber C. Kim-ball Journal, December 10, 1845; Roberts, *Comprehensive History of the Church*, 7:470-72, 541-42.

MOTHER LUCY Smith[,] the prophet Joseph's aged and honored par-ent, Wednesday, October 18, 1845 spoke in general conference. She said, "I feel that the Lord will let Brother Brigham take the people away. Here, in this city, lay dead my husband and children; and if so be the rest of my children go with you, and I would to God they may all go, they will not go without me."

–P. J. Sanders, Letter to Joseph Smith III, 4, from N. B. Lundwall, LDS Church Library.

Lucy's Conference Remarks,
October 1845

Remarks of Lucy Mack Smith, 1845, Monday, October 6, 1845.

MOTHER LUCY Smith, the aged and honored parent of Joseph Smith [arose], having expressed a wish to say a few words to the congregation. She was invited upon the stand. She spoke at considerable length and in an audible manner, so as to be heard. She commenced by saying that she was truly glad that the Lord had let her see so large a congregation. She had a great deal of advice to give. There were few in the assembly who were not acquainted with her family. She was the mother of eleven children, seven of whom were boys. She raised them in fear and love of God and never was there a more obedient family. She wished to know of the congregation, whether they considered her a mother in Israel—upon which President Brigham Young said: "All who consider Mother Smith as a mother in Israel, signify it by yes;"—one universal "yes" rang throughout.

She remarked that it was just 18 years since Joseph Smith the prophet had become acquainted with the contents of the plates, and then, in concise manner related over the most prominent points in the early history of her family, their hardships, trials, privations, persecutions, sufferings, etc.; some parts of which melted those who heard her to tears, especially the part relating to a scene in Missouri, when her beloved son Joseph was condemned to be shot in 15 minutes and she by prodigious efforts was enabled to press through the crowd to where he was, and to give him her hand. But she could not see his face; he took her hand and kissed it. She said, "Let me hear your voice once more my son." He said, "God bless you my dear mother." She gave notice that she had written her history, and wished it printed before we leave this place.

She then mentioned a discourse once delivered by Joseph, after his return from Washington, in which he said that he had done all that could be done on earth to obtain justice for their wrongs; but they were all from the president to the judge, determined not to grant justice. But, said he, keep good courage, these cases are recorded in heaven and I am going to lay them before the highest court in heaven. "Little," said she, "did I then think he was so soon to leave us to take the case up himself. And don't you think this case is being tried. I feel as though God was vexing this nation a little."

–Lucy Smith, October 8, 1845, William Berrett and Alma Burton, *Readings in LDS Church History: From Original Manuscripts* (Salt Lake City, UT: Deseret Book Company, 1955), 2: 115-116.

Lucy Mack Smith's Sermon to Nauvoo Saints, ## October 8, 1845

William Clayton, Joseph's clerk, recorded Lucy's words.

. . . [After the expulsion from Missouri] Joseph then went to the City of W[ashington]. He had a rev[elation]. to importune at the Governors feet & the Pres. Feet for the Lord said if they would not heed them he would vex the nation. After he returned he went to preaching down between Mr. Durfees [and] the Mansion house He told the brethren & sis[ters] that he had done all he could for them, says he they are determined we shall not have justice But says he keep good courage You never shall suffer for bread as you have done before. Says he all these cases is a record on earth & what is recorded here is a record in heaveny [sic]. Now says he I am a going to lay this case of their taking away our property or I am a going to take it up to the highest court in heaven. He said so 3 times—never did I think he was going to leave us so soon to take this case to heaven. He never could get justice till he took it there. I feel now just exactly that the Lord has got even the Smiths there—They know all our sufferings and don't you think our case is being tried[?] I think they will do more for us there than they could if they were here. I feel if there was no evil here [—] no talking [—] all would go right I feel that the Lo[rd] is vexing the Nation a little here & there. And I feel that the Lo[rd] will let brother Brigham take the people away. I don't know that I shall go but if W[illia]m and the rest of the family go I shall go. I feel to bless you all Brother Brigham and all Here lays my dead my husband and children. I want to lay my bones so that in the res[surection] I can rise with my husband & children. If so be that my children go with you but they will not go without me and if I go I want to have my bones fetch[ed] back to be laid with my husband & children.

–Ronald W. Walker, The Historian's Corner, "Lucy M. Smith Speaks to the Nauvoo Saints," *BYU Studies* 32, no. 1 (1991): 276-284.

–Newell and Avery, *Mormon Enigma*, 220.

In October 1845, William Smith's behavior led to his removal from the Twelve and excommunication from the Church.

"William had been living in the Mansion and now he moved his mother, Mary Bailey Smith [Samuel Smith's daughter], and two of his sisters with their husbands (Lucy and Arthur Millikin and Katherine and Jenkins Salisbury), into the vacated William Marks home with him."

William Marks's house at Nauvoo, Illinois.

Lucy and Arthur Millikin

Katharine and W. Jenkins Salisbury, W. J. Salisbury, provided courtesy of Kyle Walker.

From the time of his wife's death until his own in 1844, Lucy's son Samuel was independently raising his daughter Mary. When Samuel also passed away, Mary was left alone.

Mary began to look after Mother Smith's needs while Lucy provided invaluable companionship for the young orphan. Together, the two managed well. Lucy was able to re-establish an independent household with Mary's help.

During a November 13, 1845, prayer circle meeting, attended by Brigham Young, Heber C. Kimball, Willard Richards, George A. Smith, and Parley P. Pratt of the Twelve, along with George Miller, William W. Phelps, Orson Spencer, Lucien Woodworth, and Newel K. Whitney, "it was decided that Mother Lucy Smith should be furnished with food, clothing, and wood for the winter."

–D. Michael Quinn, *The Mormon Hierarchy: Origins of Power* (Salt Lake City, UT: Signature Books, 1994), 512.

Bishop George Miller

Owing to circumstances that developed over the next few months, Lucy never got her large, comfortable home, but Brigham did the best he could. He temporarily provided her with the spacious home of gunsmith Jonathan Browning. In April 1846 the church bought the small Joseph B. Noble residence and deeded it to Lucy.

—Newell and Avery, *Mormon Enigma*, 217.

Nauvoo Temple Work

Lucy participated in early Nauvoo Temple ordinances performed by her son Joseph. On October 8, 1843, Lucy participated in an anointing and sealing ceremony. On November 12, 1843, Joseph performed her second anointing, and also Joseph Sr.'s by proxy.

—Quinn, *Origins*, 496, 497.

Following Joseph's death, Mother Smith participated in additional temple ordinances. In 1845, church leaders reconfirmed "the holy ordinances that evening with those who have been previously mentioned as receiving them in the lifetime of the Prophet."

—Anderson, *Lucy's Book*, 785; citing Jeni Holzapfel and Richrd Holzapfel, *A Woman's view: Helen Mar Whitney's Reminiscences of Early Chruch History* (Provo, UT: BYU Religious Studies Center, 1997), 293.

Photograph of the Nauvoo Temple, ca. 1847, courtesy International Society Daughters of Utah Pioneers.

According to D. Michael Quinn,

66 **L**UCY AVOIDED further association with the Twelve thereafter, and even declined to receive from Brigham Young's hands the proxy sealing to her husband in the temple." "In the Nauvoo temple in December 1845 Mother Smith received the endowment ceremony from the hands of women who (like herself) originally received the sacred ordinances during Joseph Smith's life. She did not re-enter the Nauvoo temple in January 1846 to receive the re-performance of her marriage sealing and second anointing which she had received

directly from her son in November 1843." Lucy declined when, in 1846, Brigham Young personally re-administered those ordinances to the couples (or the surviving spouse and a proxy) who had received them from Smith.

–Quinn, *Origins*, 222, 431, fn. 199.

The *Cleveland Herald,* 1845

A correspondent of the *Albany Atlas*, writing from Nauvoo, or the "City of St. Joseph," as the Mormons style it, gives the following description of a call made upon the family of Joseph Smith:

I, of course, called upon the widow of Joe Smith, who I found a plain woman enough, without anything remarkable about her that I could observe. . . . The mother of the deceased prophet is quite another sort of a woman. The old lady is the keeper of the Egyptian mummies, and various relics and curiosities, which she exhibits to the public at two bits per head. While exhibiting the traps, the old lady gives an account of the manner of her son

Joe's finding the golden plates, and also informs the spectator that her deceased son interpreted the hieroglyphics upon the mummy cases, which figures corroborated perfectly every thing Joe had ever said, and confirmed beyond the shadow of a doubt his divine mission. She tells the same things to every visitor, and if she weeps as much with every one as she did while relating her stories to me, she would be invaluable in Broadway on a dusty day. Poor old woman, she trusts in the prophet Joseph with her whole heart.

– *The Cleveland Herald* 11 (September 13, 1845).

Lucy Mack Smith profile carved in stone.

Lucy's Portrait

—Woodruff's Journal, January 1, 1846, 3:3.

Oil portrait of Lucy Mack Smith discovered in the Mansion House attic.

William Clayton

On January 1, 1846, Wilford Woodruff presented samples of hair obtained from the Smith family to Elder Samuel Downs as a New Year's Day present. Woodruff noted in his journal that the gift included:

"**H**AIR FROM THE Heads of Joseph Smith the Prophet And all the Smith family of Male members also Mother Smith And from most all the Quorum of the Twelve Also a peace of Joseph Smith Handkerchief."

William Clayton's description of the celestial room of the Nauvoo Temple suggests that Mother Smith was in good standing with the Twelve. Clayton enumerated Lucy's portrait among various decorations. Other church leaders prominently featured included: Brigham Young, Heber C. Kimball, Orson Hyde, Willard Richards, John Taylor, George A. Smith, John Smith, and Lucius N. Scovill. The only other woman thus featured was Bathsheba B. Smith (wife of George A. Smith).

—George D. Smith, Intimate Chronicle, 206.

Miss F. J., "Visit *to* Nauvoo"

THE LADIES' MAGAZINE AND CASKET OF LITERATURE.

A non-Mormon traveler, identifying herself only as Miss F. J., published an extensive description of her 1846 visit to Nauvoo and interview with Lucy.

WHAT A JOYOUS thing it is to travel! Soon as these sunny spring-days appear, I long to don my traveling dress, turn the key of my trunk upon all necessary articles for the next three months, and throwing care to the winds, set out upon a tour that shall be as long as inclination prompts, with a purse heavy enough to balance all my wishes—tarry when I will—travel when I will—eyes and heart open wide for novelty and enjoyment. This for me, is to have a cup full of happiness to the brim.

Two years ago, this very month, the spring of 1846, I was in Quincy, Ill., with a bright warm sun shining upon me, all nature in her liveliest garb of green, and no breath of wind like that cold easterly under which I shivered half an hour ago. Nauvoo, the "City of the Saints," was not a day's sail above us,—the temple, now nearly finished, was to be dedicated on the first of May—many of us had never visited the place, and we must go now, if we would see it, before it had passed out of the hands of the Mormons, who were rapidly departing. We made up an impromptu party, and embarked on the "Ocean Wave," one of the latter days of April. We could go now in safety, for the town was crowded with speculators,—Yankees and Westerners,—buyers of land—merchants going thither with stocks of goods, to fill their pockets with money forced by necessity from the poor exiles. The supremacy of the Mormons was at an end;—but the year before, one or two distinguished gentlemen of Quincy had assured me that nothing would induce them to pass a night in Nauvoo, especially if they carried money to any amount, so desperate were the characters of the people, and so easily might a robbery, or even murder, be hushed up among them. We started at five, P. M., with sunny weather and gay hearts, enjoyed the beauties of the "lone tree prairie" on the left, and the bluffs on the right,—steamed by pretty little towns;—but before nine o'clock, were obliged to take refuge in the cabin, from the watery element those deceitful heavens showered upon us. At twelve we were wakened to hold council. It was raining as if for a second deluge;—in an hour, we should reach Nauvoo; no carriages would be on the levee at that hour;—would we go on to Burlington, with the boat, and return next day, or trust to chance for shelter for the night.

To stop at Nauvoo seemed the general wish, and when one of our number brought accounts of a poor inn just at the landing, where we could at least obtain shelter, the matter was decided. Guarded by cloaks and umbrellas, we found our way to the house, which was surrounded by boxes, barrels, furniture of various kinds, and in the shelter of the piazza sat twenty or thirty Mormons with children of all sizes, babes in the arms, waiting for morning, to cross the river. Every nook and corner of the house was occupied. The kitchen into which we were shown, was crowded also with barrels, and sleeping Mormons

Lucy's stool, shown in Maudsley's profile of Lucy in her rocking chair, coutesy L. Tom Perry Speical Collections, H. B. Lee Library, Brigham Young University.

were stretched along the floor. The only waking occupant was a crazy looking boy of twelve, a little sprig of Mormonism, whose constant occupation was plying the cooking stove with wood, and replenishing with water an immense tea-kettle; though to what purpose such assiduity, we could not surmise, as no water except in evaporation ever left it. Here then were our wretched quarters for the night, but one gentleman procured oysters, bread, and cards from the boat, and we played whist by the light of a tallow candle till morning. Then we sent off one of our gentlemen for a carriage, our only hope that it might come before breakfast, for the landlady appearing, was making bread on the same table we had seen last night covered with melted tallow, and there was not that air of purity and neatness about her person and arrangements calculated to set our hearts at ease.

"Robes loosely flowing,
hair too free."

At last, it came lumbering up to the door, an immense carriage, just as the smell of the frying bacon announced itself to our sharpened nostrils, all ready to be dished. Hungry as we were, the horses must walk a mile, through the mud; still there loomed up before the mind's eye, that comfortable hotel where all our trials would have an end.

Alas! how our hearts sank. Where was the cheerful inn-room with the bright fire [Halls—stairs, covered with mud—wild, unshaven men running about, making washstands of chairs,—ablutions anywhere,— floors covered with beds—no place of refuge but the dining-room, with floor by no means too cleanly for an Irish hovel]. We gathered up our dresses, and looked gloomily at each other:—no one had the cruelty to allude to the three days we were to pass there. The landlady appeared, mourned over her scanty accommodations;—she had taken the house only three weeks before,—had had no time to put it in order; she could hardly get food for the numbers that poured in daily upon her. She herself was a New York lady, brought up in wealth and luxury, whom change of circumstances had brought with many others to the West. My heart ached for her, but she bore a brave spirit. She would have a room above stairs made ready for us, she said, and a fire kindled as soon as possible. The prior landlord was Joe Smith, and the chamber into which we were shown had been Mrs. Smith's; some handsome articles of furniture were still remaining. We repaired our toilettes; and agreed with one voice to visit the temple, and leave Nauvoo, before the set of that day's sun. Our purposes were not changed nor modified by the influence of breakfast, at which we partook of heavy bread, and muddy coffee, with a crowd of wild scapegrace looking fellows, waited upon by dirty, slip-shod Mormon girls.

In the carriage, at length, on our way to Nauvoo, our spirits rose. Never have I seen a more lovely site for a city than that of Nauvoo. The land rises in a gradual slope of a mile from the river, and then stretches out into a vast extent of level prairie. On this elevation stands the temple, visible up and down the river for a great distance; the houses lie mostly on the slope below. There were two or three good buildings, but most were miserable log cabins. It looked like a city of paupers, and the inhabitants were a wild, squalid looking set, whose faces wore any thing but an honest, trustworthy expression. One, a desperate fellow, the perpetrator of two or three murders, for whose arrest the officers of justice were already on their way, was constantly galloping across our path to attract our attention,—his hair braided in his neck behind, with ear-rings, a purple velvet cap, and pistols in his girdle. The temple is certainly a fine building—of stone, and of great size—designed, built, and finished by the Mormons alone. There appeared to me something clumsy in its architecture, but its size

and richness strike your admiration. Poor, miserably poor as they are, as one of the Mormons observed, they yet had been able to accomplish this great and expensive building. Those who could not contribute money, gave time and labor. The hall for worship was large, but not strikingly rich, or handsome; platforms for the elders and ruling members were raised at each end, and the seats of the congregation could be turned to face either. Above, was a large hall, intended for a school-room; but the vestry below had most interest for me. The floor paved with brick, sank gradually to the centre, where stood the font, a large basin of stone, supported on the backs of twelve oxen also of stone. They were the size of life, and finely carved, with gilded horns, and ears. Each animal had a different expression. A flight of self-supporting steps led to the basin, which was large enough to hold several persons, and, passing through it, you descended by another. The effect produced upon us by these still figures, lifeless, but lifelike, in the large, silent hall, was really solemn. We climbed innumerable stairs to gain the view from the roof. It richly repaid all our trouble. Far and wide, the country revealed itself to our gaze. Below at our feet, in a half-circle, lay the little city; the Mississippi wound around us on three sides; far off, beyond it, rose the wooded shores of Missouri [Iowa]; and then, on the other side of us, back, back, far as the eye could reach, stretched the immeasurable prairie, lonely, vast, and magnificent. And every now and then, below, and on the opposite shore, and winding away in the forest, peeped out the white roofed wagon of the Mormon, conveying him and his children to a distant land. Desperate and abandoned as they were, my heart was full of sadness for them, driven out thus from their homes, and the temple of religion they had planted. But they uttered no complaints. It was their destiny, they said; not until they had raised the twelfth temple could they be permitted to settle themselves in peace. We enquired for the burial-place of the prophet, but not a Mormon would reveal it, for they believe that he is to appear again on earth, and fear lest his remains should be disturbed by the irreverent.

The next object of curiosity was Joe's mother (it seemed to us an intrusion to visit his wife.) We found a pleasant looking old lady, of seventy, or thereabouts, and to our question, "Are you the mother of the Prophet?" the mother of Washington could not have replied with greater dignity, or a prouder air. "Yes! ladies, I am the mother of the Prophet."

Her curiosities consisted of two mummy kings and their queens, who lived long before Pharaoh; also the foot of Pharaoh's daughter, and a number of sheets of hieroglyphics, which she commenced to explain. I, being seated in front of the old lady, her remarks were principally directed to me, and I sat looking into her clear, blue eyes, and wondering whether she really believed what she told us, or was conscious of her imposture. "Many years ago," she said, "a gentleman brought these hieroglyphics and mummies from Egypt. He carried the hieroglyphics to many learned men; but no one could translate them. At length, some wise professor in New York said, 'Carry them to Joe Smith, who lives at the West. He is a wise man, inspired by God. He can translate them.' And Joe did so, and found that they corresponded in every respect, with the 'Book of Mormons.'" We asked her how the Prophet received his inspiration. He was an earnest man, she said, and prayed God, night and day, to make known to him what was the true religion. One night, there was a bright-light in his chamber, which shone through the curtains of his bed, and there in his room stood the Angel of God. He told him, that the Methodist religion was no religion at all, but that if he would dig under a certain tree, he would find

Egyptian parchment

something that would teach him. Joe digged [sic] there, and found a number of plates of gold. "Did you see those plates?" I asked quickly. "No!" she answered, quietly, and severely, "but I've hefted them." It was sacrilege, it seemed, for any but the Prophet's eyes to look upon them. But Joe was not yet in a fit state to read the hieroglyphics engraved thereon, but after he had prayed for light, a long time, inspiration came. He translated them, and the Book of Mormon was published. "What did your son do then, with the plates?" I asked. "Oh! he buried them under the tree again, and the angel came, and took them." She went on, explaining the hieroglyphics, until we

were quite weary. Reason and good sense rebelled too strongly against such imposture, to make her narrations agreeable. We remunerated her for her trouble, and bade her good morning. We had no wish to wait for the dedication of the temple, or to tarry for dinner at the hotel,—but drove directly to the landing, where we expected to meet a descending boat. We did so, and soon bade adieu to Nauvoo, though the stately temple on its noble eminence long lingered in our sight. We heard after our return, that an anonymous letter was received by the commander of some troops there, advising him to search the room which had been Joe Smith's, (the same we had occupied.) There was a closet on either side of the fire-place, one of which they opened, and, removing some pegs, intended to support clothes, saw a square opening with a flight of stairs leading into the garret. This they searched, and found a place in the chimney, where a man could be concealed. They judged that there was some secret communication with the cellar, affording an avenue for escape, though they found none. I never heard whether they opened the other closet.

The Mormons left Nauvoo very soon afterward. When I visited the place a month after, on my return from Galena, it wore an air of desolation and solitude. Most of the cabins were deserted and closed. The golden light of a June sun streamed upon the quiet town, the lovely country, and majestic temple. I hope that this lovely spot may be inhabited ere long by a happy, prosperous people. The rapids below, being difficult of navigation during the summer months, its prospects however are less promising than those of Keokuk, which is situated below them.

–Miss F. J., "Visit to Nauvoo," *The Ladies' Magazine and Album [Casket of Literature]* 11 (Boston, MA: A. H. Davis, 1848), 130-36.

Nauvoo Exodus

When Church members first began to consider leaving Nauvoo for the West under the leadership of the Twelve, Lucy appeared willing to go with them. But as the time neared, she hesitated. It has been said that, Mother Smith did not go west because she felt wronged by Church trustees Almon W. Babbitt, Joseph L. Heywood, and John S. Fullmer, who refused her Church financial assistance because of her allegiance to her ex-apostle son, William.

With non-Mormons in the area growing increasingly impatient, an organized exodus began in February 1846.

IN MARCH 1846, William Smith was communicating with both the Quorum of Twelve and James Jessee Strang, seemingly playing both sides against each other. To J. J. Strang he offered the support of "the Whole Smith family," and to the Twelve he made threats and demanded . . . "a public recognition of his right as a Smith and of his office."

–Paul M. Edwards, "William B. Smith: "A Wart on the Ecclesiastical Tree," in Roger D. Launius and Linda Thatcher, eds., *Differing Visions: Dissenters in Mormon History* (Urbana, Illinois: University of Illinois Press, 1994), 148.

IN APRIL 1846, the church deeded Lucy the Joseph Bates Noble home where Lucy lived with the companionship and assistance of Mary Bailey Smith, the eight-year-old daughter of her son Samuel and her dead daughter-in-law Mary Bailey.

–Anderson, *Lucy's Book*, 786.

PER DAVID AND Della Miller, Lucy lived in the Noble house "only a few months and deeded it to Archer [Arthur] Millikin," married to her youngest daughter, Lucy.

–David E. and Della S. Miller, *Nauvoo: the City of Joseph* (Santa Barbara, California: Peregrine Smith, Inc., 1974), 215.

Noble's house, Nauvoo, Illinois.

During *the* Exodus

The Council of Twelve appointed Almon W. Babbitt, Joseph L. Heywood, and John S. Fullmer to remain in Nauvoo and manage unfinished Church business. Unhappy with how these men treated her, Lucy wrote:

March 22d, 1846.

MESSRS BABBITT, Heywood and Fullmer.

I received your letter of today, by the hand of the black boy, and I may inform you that I cannot describe my feelings when I perused its contents, such proscribed views as you have there advanced shows plainly that I am the aggrieved party, wronged as I am out of a home, long promised to me by my son, and since his death the promises were renewed all last Summer and Winter, and the last thing that Brigham said to me was, I should have a home and be provided for, in all my wants, and I think now if he were here he would not do as you have done, but you restrict my conscience, put limits to my affections, threaten me with poverty, if I do not drive my children from my door because [of] the resent insult and abuse, that has been heaped upon them without measure, but I grieve for them, I am old my feelings

are tender! Yet I must not complain. No, although my children have been the Fathers and Founders of the Church, and spent their all in its service, yea have not withheld their lives, but have been sacrificed on the altar of Mobocracy and at the feet of wicked men, have been torn from their widowed Mother. This is not enough but I am called upon to banish from my home the few of my family who are left as my only solace, as you so proudly and wickedly ask me to do, or my support shall be withheld from me, but thank kind Heaven that has implanted in my bosom affection which gold cannot buy, and which bribes cannot break the cords of, affection that binds me to the children of my bosom even eternity itself cannot break, they are interwoven with the finest arteries of my heart, and the love that flows through them is the only principle that enlivens and cheers me in this vale of tears. You would have me forsake my children in order that you may give me a living, but let it not be said that in the Church of Jesus Christ of Latter Day Saints, a mother has to forfeit all natures ties, to cut asunder the cords of affection that bind her to her children, or she shall not have a subsistence. Tell it not to the World, let it not be heard among natures sons of the forest. I think no Christian Spirit could have dictated such cold charity to me or any one who merits other treatment. A headless body has no life you say, but it may have pockets into which the head when in its place put the means of my subsistence. I do look for help some way. Provide me a house and do as you think best, if I suffer more my God will plead my cause, something must be done for Spring is coming on. As to the head of the Church I am Mother and ask obedience to the Law of God, and all will be right and none that feel as Joseph did will wrong his Mother, his Brother, or his Sisters. What is done I would like to have done immediately. Give me a deed to a house and lot and advance the Quarterly sum. A part of my family have left me today and I expect William to begone soon and he will go and come as the Lord directs him. I wish to be cultivating a garden soon, I have no means, no food but coarse corn meal and I am old and feeble in health—Will you call and see me and talk on these affairs[?] As to William he is my son and he has rights. As to the twelve you say they have rights, but who shall decide between them. Are you the judge. The Twelve speak against William, and William speaks in his own defence.

You say he slanders them, he says they have slandered him and robbed him of his rights and done other things as well but I shall leave these things to one who is a just God and will measure to all men their just deserts in the day of accounts. As to the merits of my children none are more worthy to have an inheritance in the city of Joseph and you are now living on the labor of their hands. I will not speak of this further, as it excites my tender feelings, to think that any should be so heartless as to consider that after their labors for years in sickness, in persecution, and perils by sea and land, and suffering privations and the loss of all thing[s] to protect the Prophet my son and build up the Kingdom of God, and now they are not worthy of an inheritance. O shame! where is thy blush? Let this be a sufficient rebuke from your Mother in Israel, Amen. Lucy Mack Smith Mother in Israel.

P. S.—Can it be possible that I shall be driven to the necessity of calling upon others, or looking to another source for help, God forbid.

—Lucy Smith, Letter to Babbitt, Heywood and Fullmer, March 22, 1846, published in *Voree Herald* 1, no. 8 (August 1846): 35.

James J. Strang

James J. Strang.

James J. Strang, a Latter Day Saint from Wisconsin, emerged as the most serious contender among several potential successors to challenge the leadership claims of the Twelve. Strang succeeded in winning a significant number of early church members and leaders to his cause.

Apostle John E. Page is one such individual. In a letter to Strang, Page confided:

I THEREFORE SAY IN true sincerity of heart.... that I am fully persuaded by the word of the Lord, and the spirit of truth, that you are the man to fill the place of Joseph Smith, as prophet—Revelator—Seer—and Translator to the Church, and discharge all, and several the duties that involved [devolved up]on Pres-Smith.

–John E. Page, Letter to James J. Strang, March 12, 1846, CofC Archives.

After his excommunication by the Twelve, William Smith was also attracted to James Strang's movement.

Strang courted the Smith family, addressing several letters to Emma. While living at the Mansion, William encountered Strang's letters. William replied to Strang by sharing his perception of the standing of the Smith family at Nauvoo.

Nauvoo, March 11, 1846

ROTHER STRANG:

I have perused with becoming interest your several letters sent to my mother and sister Emma; also some of your papers with your remarks on the order of the church, which clearly evinces the true sprirt of old Mormonism as far as I can discern the faith and doctrine that I have been advocating for years, and for which, of late my family (mother Smith not excepted) have been disfranchised from the church (as they call it) BY THE TWELVE, and much abused by their infatuated followers. Time would fail me to mention all of the accumulated wrongs they have inflicted upon a poor and helpless family, whose members have mostly fallen by the hand of a ruthless mob and the treachery of false hearted brethren. A few yet remain to suffer by confiscation of their goods; their rights of church property taken from them, until the bleeding heart of an aged mother wrung with anxiety & disgust sinks with anguish, and faints at the thoughts of a recital of the awful tale. Hear it, O ye Latter Day Saints: Your Mother in Israel, who oft-times has nursed you at her side, and with her motherly care and teaching comforted your hearts, must now be driven from your midst, penniless—robbed of her inheritance in the city of Joseph by the cruelty of your rulers.

On yesterday we were told by a committee of two, a Mr. Babbit[t] and a Mr. Haywood, that unless we would acknowledge the Twelve as the heads of the church, Mother Smith could have no inheritance in Nauvoo. . . . My mother and family in general join with me in sending their love to you and all the saints scattered abroad. We shall all leave this place (Nauvoo) for some more heavenly land.

–William Smith, Nauvoo, Illinois, Letter to James J. Strang, March 11, 1846, *Voree Herald* 1, no. 4 (April 1846), 19.

In a March 1, 1846, communication, apparently also signed by Lucy and other members of the Smith family, William pledged support for James Strang's succession claim. The statement appeared in the July 1846 issue of Strang's *Voree Herald*:

THIS IS TO CERTIFY that the Smith family do believe in the appointment of J. J. Strang.

William Smith, Patriarch
Lucy Smith, Mother in Israel
Arthur R. Milliken
Nancy [sic] Milliken
W. J. Salisbury
Catherine Salisbury
Sophronia McLerie
Nauvoo, March 1st, 1846

–William Smith, "I have since I returned to Nauvoo," *Voree Herald*, 1, no. 7 (July 1846): 31.

Nauvoo Broadside

Perhaps concerned that he was losing a public relations battle with the Twelve and eager to prove that he was best able to look after his mother's interests, William B. Smith distributed a broadside reading:

TO THE PUBLIC.

THE FOLLOWING document, which was signed and delivered in the presence of A. W. Babbitt Esq., will show how much honesty, sincerity, or good faith there is in Wm. Smith's pretended claims to any portion of the Church property. In the first place, he had no claim: But, to avoid any difficulty or contention, the Trustees agreed to give to his mother the property mentioned in the following.

TO ALL TO WHOM THIS MAY CONCERN:

THIS IS TO CERTIFY, that we, the members of the Smith family, in consideration of Mother Smith have received from the Church of Jesus Christ of Latter-day Saints, a deed of conveyance of a house and lot in the city of Nauvoo, Hancock county; built and occupied by Joseph B. Noble, valued, in ordinary times, at the sum of twelve hundred dollars. We hereby in consideration of the above named and mentioned donation, and deed of conveyance, declare ourselves perfectly satisfied with the dealings of said church with Mother Smith; and freely acknowledge that the said church is hereby released from all moral and legal obligation to us or either of us.

In testimony whereof, we have hereunto set our hands, this thirteenth day of April, in the year of our Lord one thousand eight hundred and forty six, at Nauvoo, Hancock county, Illinois.

WM. SMITH,
ARTHUR MILLIKIN,
LUCY MILLIKIN.

–William Smith et. al., "To All To Whom This May Concern," Nauvoo, Illinois, April 13, 1846, Chicago Historical Society; Typescript P96, f77, CofC Archives.

State Troops in Nauvoo, 1846

In late April 1846, as state riflemen from Quincy were preparing to withdraw from Carthage, Illinois, Major Warren decided to retain a small force at Nauvoo to keep the peace and see that the Mormons performed their agreement to leave. Accordingly a detachment consisting of Captain Morgan, Lieutenants Prentiss and Henry, Sergeants Hunt, Evans, and Everitt, with Privates Carlin, Bush, Peck and Grant went to Nauvoo where Major Warren joined them and they were quartered at the house of Joseph Smith's widow.

THEY FOUND HER a sensible woman, and the son of the prophet an intelligent lad. He was about fourteen years old and afterward claimed the succession. The prophet's mother was also living, although very aged. Her duty and delight was to exhibit an interminable roll of sere cloth said to have been taken from a mummy, which was covered with hieroglyphics and figures that she undertook to explain in a mumbling voice. The only intelligible words being the oft-repeated statement, "It all goes to prove the Book of Mormon true."

–Cora Agnes Bennison, "The Quincy Riflemen in Mormon War, 1844-46," Lecture, *The Quincy Daily Whig* (May 26, 1909); cited in John C. Grainger, "A Visit to Historic Places," *Journal of History* 3, no. 2 (April 1909): 214-15.

In May 1846, William advised Rueben Hedlock in England that "the whole Smith family . . . excepting Hyrum's widow uphold Strang, and say this wilderness move is not of God." This letter was accompanied by one from Lucy to Hedlock on May 11, 1846.

Nauvoo, May 11th 1846.

MY DEAR SON,

For so I must call you; as there is little time left me, I will be brief—The church has passed through much affliction, and it pains my heart that it should suffer more. The Twelve (Brighamites) have abused my son William, and trampled upon my children; they have also treated me with contempt. The Lord's hand is in this to save the church; now mark it; these men are not right, God has not sent them to lead this kingdom; I am satisfied that Joseph appointed J. J. Strang. It is verily so. Now Brother Ruben I exhort you for the love you bear for the truth to hear my voice, and warn the Saints concerning these things, and your reward shall be double in the heavenly worlds. This from your mother,

Lucy Smith, Mother in Israel.

Arthur and Lucy Milliken, and W. Jenkins and Catharine

Salisbury signed the postscript certifying "that We the undesigned [sic] members of the Smith family fully accord with the sentiments expressed above."

–Lucy Mack Smith, Letter to Rueben Hedlock, Nauvoo, Illinois, May 11, 1846, *Voree Herald* 1, no. 6 (June 1846): 25.

A postscript to a letter to Strang, described Lucy's alleged treatment by the Twelve.

May 1846, Nauvoo, Illinois

BROTHER STRANG:

I forgot to mention that many have sent presents of purses, with money, shawls, c[l]othes &c &c. from England & the different states to the mother of the Prophet but she has not received any of them in consequence of [Orson] Hyde & others telling them it was dangerous to call on Mother Smith, & they might not to do it, but go right strait [sic] across the [Mississippi] river.

Wm Smith
Lucy Smith Mother in Israel

–William Smith, Letter to James J. Strang, May 1846, Nauvoo, Illinois, Typescript, P13, f65, CofC Archives.

All those wishing to leave Nauvoo were not able to do so immediately. Later in the year, Hyrum Smith's widow, Mary Fielding Smith, now a plural wife of Heber C. Kimball, completed her own preparations to travel west. Her daughter Martha Ann remembered, on September 8, 1846, "We left our home just as it was, our furniture, and the fruit trees hanging full of rosy cheeked peaches. We bid goodbye to the loved home that reminded us of our beloved father every where we turned. ... We bid goodbye to our dear old feeble grandmother [Lucy Mack Smith]."

–Martha Ann [Smith] Harris, Centennial Jubilee Letter, March 22, 1881. Quoted in Don C. Corbett, *Mary Fielding, Daughter of Britain* (Salt Lake City, Utah: Deseret Book Company, 1966), 195.

Lucy's Move *to* Knox County, Illinois

Initially, Emma and Lucy hoped to remain in Nauvoo throughout the Mormon exodus. But, as anti-Mormon feelings swelled throughout the Illinois countryside, everyone associated with the Mormons in any way was eventually forced to leave.

James Blanchard, who was in Nauvoo following the September 1846 Battle of Nauvoo described conditions via letter to William Smith:

November 6, 1846

I HAVE JUST ARRIVED here from the [scene] of action & take this opportunity to write you. ... So much confusion for the last two or three weeks the way the Mormons have shelled out of Nauvoo is a sight I hope not to see many such scen[e]s Mont-Rose & all Iowa is perfectly lined with them women & children suffering beyond endureance.

–James L. Blanchard, Letter to William Smith, Oquawka, Illinois, November 6, 1846, Yale University, Typescript, P96, f77, CofC Archives.

Emma withdrew from Nauvoo taking her family for a time to Fulton, Illinois.

ALONG WITH her daughter Lucy [Millikin] and her daughter's husband Arthur Millikin, Lucy remained in the Noble house for a few months until the 1846 Battle of Nauvoo forced them to flee the city. For a time, Lucy resided near Galesburg, Knox County, Illinois with the Millikins. William B. Smith also made his home nearby.

–Ronald E. Romig, *Emma's Nauvoo* (Independence, MO: John Whitmer Books, 2007), 31.

Mary Hancock, a 20th century descendant of Mother Lucy, reminisced,

LUCY SMITH [Millikin] (youngest sister of Joseph Smith the Prophet) . . . lived with Lucy Mack Smith after <her son> Joseph's death. . . [and] moved [during the Exodus from Nauvoo] with many other Saints to Colchester leaving Lucy's mother (Lucy Mack Smith) & a granddaughter Mary Bailey Smith with Joseph's wife, Emma Hale Smith, for a short time[.] But <Mother> Lucy Mack Smith not being contented & who had mostly lived with her younger daughter Lucy went to Colchester taking her granddaughter Mary Bailey <with> her where she lived for several years.

–Mary Hancock, Letter to Israel A. Smith, August 27, 1956, original, P13, f2126, CofC Archives.

According to Mormon historian Stanley B. Kimball, Mother Smith took the mummies and papyri with her to Knox County. Lucy eventually returned to Nauvoo during 1847 to live with her daughter-in-law, Emma Smith. There is no evidence that she ever possessed or exhibited the mummies after returning to Nauvoo.

William apparently acquired Lucy's mummies believing they "would strengthen his claim to leadership among the Mormons who did not follow Brigham Young west."

On December 2, 1846, William assured James J. Strang that "the mummies and records are safe." In a follow-up letter on December 19, 1846, William told Strang he was planning to bring them to Strang's headquarters at Voree, Wisconsin. Two years later, Almon W. Babbitt writing to Brigham Young from Nauvoo, January 31, 1848, noted, "Wil-

liam [still] has got the mummies from Mother Smith and refuses to give them up." . . . Because of William's acute poverty, he may have leased or sold them to a traveling exhibitor of curiosities, "A. Combs," with the option to repurchase later, possibly as a condition imposed by Lucy.

–Stanley Kimball, "New Light on Old Egyptana," *Dialogue* 6, no. 4 (Winter 1983): 84-85, 86, 89.

William B. Smith, courtesy Kyle Walker.

Voree

William visited Voree, Wisconsin, where he was ordained an apostle and patriarch in

Voree, Wisconsin, historical marker.

Strang's church.

While there, William announced plans to build a house for Lucy in Voree and solicited funds to help with her move.

–Anderson, *Lucy's Book*, 788-89.

In December, William advised James Strang,

THE REASON I DID not attend the conference [was because] I was sick at Perkins Grove. . . After my health had recovered sufficiently and on hearing that my folks was at Knoxville I hastened to give them council. . . I found my Mother 2 Sisters and their families—at the house of Brother Padems all—stowed into a room about 15—by 12 feet with only a small grate fire Place to Cook by—In this condition—they have been living for 4 weeks waiting for help and teams from Voree. About this time Brother Galand called on us and said he thought it would be the best thing [for us] . . . to rent houses and stay the winter and not go to Voree Untill Spring. This I thought most advisable as Mother was old and very much cripled up with the rheumatism and [going] to Voree in the cold—this late season of the year would Endanger her life. I have now got her a Comfortable room for the winter. I am also keeping house by myself.

–William Smith, Letter to James J. Strang, Knoxville, Illinois, December 7, 1846, Yale University; Typescript P96, f77, CofC Archives.

A week later, William informed Strang that his family was ready to travel to Voree,

AS EARLY IN THE spring as the trailing will permit say about the first of April. To remove us it will require 7 teams, and one extra Carriage for Mother Smith to ride in. She is quite fee-

ble and I feel anxious that she may be removed to Voree and see the Prophet before . . . she is—gathered to the Land of her fathers. The mummies & records are with us and will be of benefit to the Church [if] we Can get them to Voree. Mother has also the history of her life written and Prepared for the Press. In getting out of Nauvoo Mother has left all and sold her horses & Carriage to pay Expences so that She has nothing now to help herself and is one reason why I am so particular in—speaking of the amount of help and the kind &c. &c. We shall need some money also in trailing on the road. I have written in time that the Church may know, thinking perhaps that I may not be in this part of the cuntrey when this information would be wanting.

–William Smith, Letter to James J. Strang, Knoxville, Illinois, December 19, 1846, Yale University; Typescript, P96, f77, CofC Archives.

A falling-out occurred before the Smiths could move to Voree. Soon after, *The Racine*, (Wisconsin), *Advocate* newspaper, carried a report "that Lucy Smith, the mother in Israel of the Mormons, and the rest of the Jo. Smith family, insist, that they

do not believe that Strang of Voree, was ever appointed a prophet by Jo. Smith."

–"Can't Get the Papers," *Racine Advocate* 4, no. 43 (September 16, 1846).

William B. Smith.

In the end, conformity to Strang's system proved too difficult and in October 1847, William was excommunicated by Strang in absentia "for adultery and apostasy."

After his encounter with Strang, William declared himself president of his own movement. Isaac Sheen, of Cincinnati, Ohio, published the *Melchisedek and Aaronic Herald* in support of William's claims.

In April 1847, as the Twelve headed west, they addressed a long letter to the mother of the Prophet. It began,

Winter Quarters, April 4, 1847

BELOVED MOTHER in Israel, Our thoughts, our feelings, our desires and our prayers to our Heavenly Father, in the name of Jesus, are often drawn out in your behalf. ... We are speedily to depart from this place, with other pioneers, and go westward over the mountains, as we shall be led by the spirit of the Lord, to find a location for a stake of Zion, we felt that we could not take our leave without addressing a line to Mother Smith, to let her know that her children in the Gospel have not forgotten her. ... If our dear Mother Smith should at any time wish to come where the Saints are located, and she will make it manifest to us, there is no sacrifice we will count too great to bring her forward, and we ever have been, now are and shall continue to be, ready to divide with her the last loaf.

–Quorum of Twelve, Letter to Lucy Mack Smith, April 4, 1847, William Berrett and Alma Burton, *Readings in LDS Church History* (Salt Lake City, UT: Deseret Book Company, 1955), 2: 194-196.

Lyman Wight

Soon, William and Sheen became involved with Lyman Wight, who was in Texas. Lyman addressed the following letter to Lucy:

Zodiac Mills, [Texas],
August 21, 1848

MOTHER SMITH I received a copy of a letter last evening written by your son William and handed to me from William P. Eldridge, in answer to a letter written from Almon Babbit[t] and others. The answer was sweet to my taste and the most consoling that I have had for many years.

Mother Smith, I am well aware of the tribulations you had in losing your oldest son, about the time that brother Joseph, in his infancy, was striving to bring forth salvation for this the seventh and last dispensation of God on earth. Then your companion of seventy years of age, one of the greatest Patriarchs that ever lived on the face of the earth. You have since in an hour been deprived of your youngest son by a mortal disease. Not more than two years from that time you was deprived of Joseph the prophet, seer, and revelator of this dispensation, and Hyrum who was the Patriarch under his father's hands. In a few weeks after that you was deprived of Samuel one of the most noble sons among the children of men. Alas! Shall I say in the space of a few years, is it possible that you was deprived of sons the most noble of all the earth, and left with one son and three daughters to mourn the loss of five of the most affectionate sons that were ever born of a woman. And after all Mother Smith, you been asked to turn the last son you have on earth, who was appointed an apostle by Joseph who is the Prophet, seer, and revelator of the last dispensation of God on earth, from your door and forbid him a home. From whom were you asked this, from aspirants, from monarchs, or from the most abusive of all men on earth.

Orson Hyde, a poor little pusillanimous know nothing, has endeavored to write largely against me. Who is Orson Hyde? He is a man whom Joseph sent with John Gould to Independence to see about our internal affairs. They stopped with us a day or two when the mob broke out. Orson Hyde immediately repaired to a boat at the Independence landing, three miles from Independence, where we had concentrated to meet the mob. He wrote an inflammatory letter concerning a heavy fight having taken place, in which he thought there was two or three hundred killed, when not a gun had been fired on either side. When did we next hear from Orson Hyde? It was when Tom B. Marsh had written a letter to the Governor of Missouri, informing him that the Mormons were hacking, hewing and destroying every thing before them, burning houses and turning the inhabitants out of doors, which was a lie.—Orson Hyde signed his name to the letter and then run as all cowards do run. When did we next see Orson Hyde? In the city of Washington, when he was sent by Br. Joseph, to obtain, if possible, a charter for Br. Joseph to get 250,000 men to secure our rights and privileges upon the confines of Mexico and in the Cordillera mountains in the state of Texas. He wrote back to Br. Joseph that his name was unpopular, and would fain have put his little pusillanimous name in his stead, for which Br. Joseph sharply rebuked him in a letter which I carried to him with my own hands. Where is Orson Hyde now? In the Eastern states, begging the coppers from dead negroes [sic] eyes to support his claim of infamous rascality, while he pretended to be a saint of the Most High God, and reproaching the Smith family who have most gloriously and triumphantly brought forth the seventh and last dispensation of God on earth for the salvation of the human family.

Mother Smith we would inform you that in addition to our little company of 150 souls who left Nauvoo, our numbers have increased to 240, made up of numbers in the state of Texas, who are all as anxious for your welfare as I am, myself. And we took a joint resolution today of the whole body that you should stand as John said Mary stood when he was on the isle of Patmos. She had a crown of gold upon her head and twelve stars in that crown. And that you are the mother of the Angel of the seventh and last dispensation of God on earth. And we believe that your ripened years should secure you a living from the hands of those of whom you are the Mother, and we thank God that in coming to Texas we have been able to give you a liberal support, either in Nauvoo or in Texas as shall seem you good, and that William your last and only son that is left upon the earth, and who is the Patriarch of the church of the Most High God, shall share abundantly in your blessings, we knowing as we do that he is worthy of all acceptation. As to Brigham we have nothing to say farther than said to Alexander the copper smith "the Lord reward him according to his deeds." To Emma we say that whilst our hands are able to labor she shall never lack for support, although we expect she is more able to support herself than we are to support her, yet we have the best of feelings toward her, and to young Joseph we say it is your privilege to take your father's place, and to this we will all give head [heed] universally, but if you think it beneath your privilege some of your younger brethren must come in according to the decree of Almighty God. Mother Smith fear not we shall communicate often.

To my Son Orange.—I glory in your spirit to do the will of God on earth, never cease to do his will, neither cease to labor with the Smith family as long as there is one remaining upon the face of the earth. Tell William I respect him as a friend and a brother in Christ Jesus our Lord, that according to his address his mind is perfectly right. Tell Mother Smith that I shall never forget the day nor the hour that we crossed the lake together. Tell Emma that I shall never forget nor forsake her, for Joseph was my father, my life and my friend. Tell young Joseph that if he did but know it his calling is as high as the heavens, and when Jackson County is redeemed he will be the sole proprietor in building the Temple of the Great God until his father is resurrected from the dead.

Now my son Orange, eight times have I left home since I was ordained an elder and been gone from six to eight months at a time. Let not your mind fall beneath that of your fathers. We would be glad to see you, but we would be more glad to know that the feeble and transitory things of this world had not drawn your mind from that glorious principle of the service you could be to the human family.

I remain your father as ever, a child to Mother Smith, a brother to Joseph and Emma, and all the remaining part of the family, and with due respect I greet the whole family universally.   Lyman Wight

–Lyman Wight, Letter to Lucy Mack Smith, August 21, 1848, *The Melchisedek and Aaronic Herald* 1, no. 3 (May 1849): 4.

Orson Hyde

Orson Hyde.

Isaac Sheen, editor of William Smith's periodical, published Wight's and William's letters in his short-lived *Melchisedek and Aaronic Herald* in Covington, Kentucky, during the spring and summer of 1849. This generated a blistering response from Orson Hyde, who was then editing the *Frontier Guardian* in Kanesville, Iowa. On November 14, 1849, he reported that William had accused church leaders of "oppressing and wronging" Lucy "out of a living." Hyde first denounced William as lazy, violent, and so immoral that his good opinion of another "may be regarded as a strong presumptive evidence of like depravity," then pointedly as-

serted that it was William's job, not Brigham Young's, to support Lucy:

WE PROPOSED TO furnish Mother Smith a comfortable house, free of rent, and to settle upon her one hundred and fifty dollars yearly for life; and to pay her quarterly in advance: Mr. Babbitt is a witness to this transaction or proposal, for it was made through him. William, at this time, was his mother's adviser. He was opposed to her accepting it, and concluded that the Church would go so far away that they would never pay the installments; and William thought it best to make as large a grab, at once, as he could, and let the rest go. It was, therefore, Williams advice, and the old lady's conclusion to ask the Church to purchase for her a house and lot, that she might have a home that she could call her own. She selected her house and lot and it was agreed by her and William that if the Church would buy that house and lot and give her a deed of it, they would release the Church from any farther obligation for Mother Smith's support. We told them that they were unwise, and would probably rue their course: But they insisted, and nothing else would satisfy.

We went and borrowed the gold

and paid it over to Mr. Joseph R. [B.] Noble, four hundred dollars, for his house and lot, and he, Noble, executed a deed of the premises to Mother Smith where she has resided from that time till the present; and by diligence and close financiering, we have succeeded in repaying all.

These are the facts of the case, and if William does not remember the whole circumstances, we will refresh his memory. It was just about the time that he made application to us through Mr. Babbitt to come back into the Church; but the conditions of his coming back among the apostate Brighamites as he calls us, were too severe upon him. They were, that he go to work like an honest man and support himself by his own industry. That he cease to be idle and learn to tell the truth and to be a virtuous upright man. These were burthens too grievous for him to bear, and the prospect being so gloomy, that he concluded to say that he never made any such application. . . .

Shame on a man, in the prime of life that will whine because somebody else will not support his mother!

–"Mother Smith," *The Frontier Guardian* 1, no. 21 (November 14, 1849): 1.

Almon W. Babbit, courtesy International Society Daughters of Utah Pioneers.

Joseph B. Noble.

William McLellin, 1847

William E. McLellin, courtesy Church Archives, The Church of Jesus Christ of Latter-day Saints.

Lucy was in Nauvoo in late 1847 when William McLellin stopped by. McLellin's visit with Lucy is described in his periodical, *The Ensign of Liberty*, published at Kirtland, Ohio.

ON OUR WAY [home from a visit to church sites in Missouri] we called at the city of Nauvoo again, and visited while there, that superb structure, "the Nauvoo Temple." We also visited old mother Smith, and found her very feeble indeed, from age, hardships, exposures, and sorrows. Her faith and confidence in her religion, seemed only to have gathered strength by the varying vicissitudes through which she has passed during a long life. She took great interest in rehearsing matters combined with the death of her sons. I must say that I walked mournfully through the fated city of desolations.

–William E. McLellin, "Our Apology—and Our Tours," *The Ensign of Liberty* 1, no. 3 (December 1847): 34.

Failing Health, 1849

In a letter to William Smith, datelined "Nauvoo, the 4th of January, 1849," Lucy complains, "I am sick and feeble."

Nauvoo,
the 4th of January, 1849

MY DEAR SON William, These letters I received the same time I received yours which I send you. I received your letter dated Philadelphia, December, 1848, which gave me consolation to hear that you are alive, and building up the cause of our Heavenly Father, and I hope the Lord will prosper you.

I am sick and feeble. I hope you will write as quick as you get this. They all join me in sending their love to you.

This from your mother.

Lucy Smith

–Lucy Smith, Nauvoo, Illinois, Letter to William Smith, January 4, 1849, *Melchisedek and Aaronic Herald* 1, no. 2 (March 1849): 1.

Based upon a letter from Jenkins Salisbury, William Smith, and Isaac Sheen described Lucy's health as precarious in August 1849, in the *Melchisedek and Aaronic Herald*.

MOTHER SMITH, mother of the martyred prophets, Joseph and Hiram [sic] Smith has been sick, nigh unto death, and although she has recovered, it is not expected that she will live long. This information we have obtained by a letter which the prophet William has just received from his brother-in-law W. J. Salisbury.

The Brighamite leaders have not only broken their promise to assist Mother Smith, but have unjustly deprived her of property which belonged to her. It has been their determination to impoverish the Smith family, and to chastise them, as they say, until they will consent to unite with them. This avowal has been made to us by one of their leaders.

Saints of the last days, will you not assist mother Smith by pecuniary aid, without delay. The blessings of the God of Joseph, Hyram [sic] and William will rest upon you for so doing. Let the consideration of the blessings which you have received through her labors arouse you to perform an act of gratitude toward her now. Mother Lucy Smith resides at Nauvoo, Hancock Co., Ill. Letters and remittances directed to her, post paid will be thankfully received,

Wm. Smith
I. Sheen Pres[idents]

—"Mother Smith," *Melchisedek and Aaronic Herald* 1, no. 5 (August 1849): 4.

After visiting Lucy, family friend John Bernhisel reported to Brigham Young,

66 **M**OTHER SMITH'S health is very feeble, and in all human probability she will not survive another winter." Bernhisel also reported to Young that Lucy "inquired after you and others."

—John Bernhisel, New York, Letter to Brigham Young, September 10, 1849, Young Manuscript letters, 245-46, LDS Church Library.

In September 1849, Smith and Sheen advised readers:

WE HAVE ALSO ONE [a letter] from Bro. H. Herinshaw, Nauvoo, which states that the health of Mother Smith is improved.

—"Letter from Pres. Wm. Smith," *Melchisedek and Aaronic Herald* 1, no. 6 (September 1849): 1.

In 1849, William Smith wrote to Lyman Wight. William's letter contained news about Lyman's son, Orange, and also a reference to Lucy.

Orange Wight.

BRO. ORANGE WAS AT my place in Palestine, Ill., some time in August or the first of September last [1848], in good spirits. He stayed at my house and in the neighborhood some five or six days. He brought us good news from a far country, and refreshed our spirits much. He also went to see Mother Smith in Nauvoo. In that place I first met with him while on his visit among us. He left my place, Palestine, in company with a family, and expected to accompany several more on their way to Texas, with many good wishes and good blessings for his safe arrival in the valley of his home. Many more who were left behind would have been glad to have gone along, and did not feel much like staying behind. God bless you Bro. Wight, for such is the word of the Lord to me, Amen.

W. S.

–William Smith, Letter to Lyman Wight, April 21, 1849, *Melchisedek and Aaronic Herald* 1, no. 4 (June 1849): 2.

"Mother Lucy, daughter Lucy, and family moved to Webster in Hancock county in the fall of 1849. Two years later, they moved to Fountain Green. Granddaughter Mary Bailey Smith was with Lucy all of this time."

–Anderson, *Lucy's Book*, 791.

In the early 1850s, Mother Smith moved back to Nauvoo and spent the remainder of her life living with Emma's family. Toward the end of her life, Lucy suffered from severe arthritis and spent much of her time in a wheelchair or in bed.

With Emma Again

Apparently, Lucy returned to Emma's home in April 1852.

Julia Murdock Smith Dixon Middleton.

Julia Murdock Smith Middleton, anticipated the occasion in a letter to Emma:

YOU SAY GRAND Mother is coming to live with you I am glad to here it It will Seeam[sic] like old times once more wont It altho It will bee a great burthern to you how I wish I was there to help you.

–Julia M. Dixon, Letter to Emma Smith Bidamon, March 25, 1852, Lewis C. Bidamon Papers, P12-2, f17, CofC Archives.

Mormon visitors to Nauvoo throughout "the early 1850s frequently called on 'Mother Smith,' and she always greeted them with pleasure and affection."

–Anderson, *Lucy's Book*, 793.

Perrigrine Sessions, 1852

Perrigrine Sessions.

Lucy was living with Emma when Perrigrine Sessions, son of David and Patty Sessions, boarded overnight in the Nauvoo Mansion House, November 29-30, 1852. Session's expanded contemporary diary reads:

CROST THE Mississippi river to Nauvoo put up to [t]he Mansion house [30 Nov.] saw the mother of the Prophet Joseph she was quite feble but recollected me and apered quite glad to see me saw Emmy the prophets Wife and his mother she was glad to hear my voice but could not see me Emma seamed verry cool and indifferent and though so well aquainted in the days gone by seamed to bee a stranger to me and to that spirit [that] caracturized her and the Prophet when he lived and she has four children but looked as though of atruth they were without a father they once had every thing looked gloomy about the mansion the spirit of God has departed Nauvoo and the home of the Prophet.

–Donna Toland Smart, *Mormon Midwife: the 1846-88 Diaries of Patty Bartlett Sessions* (Logan, UT: Utah State University, 1997), 166-67.

James Allen

James X. Allen's British LDS emigrant party stopped at Nauvoo in 1853. James described an interesting visit with Lucy.

N THE LAST DAY of April I went to Nauvoo, & beheld the disolate Citty

Nauvoo Temple Ruins.

once the pride & delight of the people of God; & the remains of the beautiful white stone temple situated at the summit of the hill & viewed with mingled feelings of pleasure & sorrow delighted in being previlaged to gaze upon the house dedicated to the Lord & in which he had bestowed great blessings on its saints. In giving unto them his most holy spirit with the precious gift of the priesthood after the order of Jesus the humble Nazereen, now seated at the righted hand of the heavens <his> father in the heavens, but sorry to behold it in its ruined state & to be looked on by the eyes of the ungodly; & that too with feelings of triumph over the exiled sons & daughters of Israel. Though, the temple is beautiful even in its ruins; & its magnificence, & bold front stands with its head towring towards

the bleue skiy as though biding defiance to its enemies, & looking with Contempt upon its unrighteious neighbors, & viles intentions upon the consecrated soil of the people of God. After looking over the Citty & rainging through the Nauvoo house, I went to the house builded by the Prophet a short time prier to his marterdom, now a temperance Hotel & keeped by Major Batterman [Bidamon] who has taken to wife the prophet Joseph's widow. I had a short conversation with Mrs. Batterman & was introduced to old Mother Smith who lay sick in bed, but on my being introduced to her She raised herself up in bed & extended her hand to me asking if I came from England & were I purposing going to the valley to live with the Mormons; I answered in the affirmative at which she appeared somewhat surprised & asked me if I could not make my [home] in that neighborhood, or, in some of the neiboring states, she stated land was cheape & the soil rich, & that work was pleantiful & wages good, & that I might serve the Lord there as well as any where else. She talked much about Brigham Young & the people who follow him, stating that the former was an Usurper, & was pronounced by her Son while alive, & in her hearing, she also spoke much against polygamy & produced a pasage from the book of mormon to prove it false, the old lady was much affected & spoke warmly oure conversation lasted for the space of an hour & an halfe—when I left & whent to Mont Rose & there remained all night.

–James X. Allen, Journal fragment, 1853, Burgess Papers, P109, f59, CofC Archives.

Lucy remained part of Emma's family until her death. Mary Bailey Smith provided care for Lucy until she married Edward Kelteau in late 1854 or early 1855. After this, much of the burden inevitably fell upon Emma.

James Ririe, 1853

James Ririe, part of an emigrant party passing through Nauvoo en route to Utah in 1853, wrote,

NEXT NIGHT WE landed at Keokuk so our sailing was done with. We lay three days at Keokuk and then started for the plains. Such bad roads I have never seen. We went 13 miles from Keokuk and lay over. We lightened up and burnt boxes and goods. I threw away about 100 pounds of clothing, etc.

On Sunday, about twenty of us went across the Mississippi River to Nauvoo. We saw the ruins of the Saints' homes, the ruins of the Temple and we visited the Nauvoo Mansion. We saw Mr. Bidamon, the man who married Emma Smith. We saw Lucy Smith, the Prophet's mother, and also Emma. We also saw his three sons, Joseph, Frederick, and David. David was then in his 9th year and Joseph was 21. We also saw Mr. Bidamon's little girl about the same age as David. They were all playing together about the house.

–James Ririe, in Kate B. Carter, ed., *Our Pioneer Heritage*, 9 (1966): 338-75.

Hannah King, 1853

On May 12, 1853, British convert Hannah Tapfield King called on the family. She found Lucy

"**P**ILLOWED UP in bed but alert and articulate. She is a splendid old lady, and my heart filled up at sight of her—She blessed us with a mother's blessing, her own words, and bore her testimony to the work

Lewis Bidamon, courtesy Liberty Hall.

of the last days, and to Joseph Smith as a prophet of the Lord. . . my heart melted for I remembered my own dear mother left in England for the gospel's sake, and the deep fountains of my heart were broken up. ... Lucy made a great impression on me for she is no ordinary woman. ... she is a character that Walter Scott would have loved to portray and he would have done justice to her.

—Journal and Reminiscence of Hannah Tapfield King, May 12, 1853, Holograph, MS 1573, LDS Church Library.

Brother *and* Sister Bona

Samuel Walker related a story of Brother and Sister Bona's 1853 interview with Lucy:

Austin, Nevada,
September 23, 1869.

BRO. JOSEPH:
I passed the day, last Sabbath, with Father Bona and family. They were in Nauvoo in 1853, and saw Grandmother Lucy at the Nauvoo House. Sister Bona sung, "Hail to the Prophet." "Grandma" asked them if they knew that Joseph Smith was a prophet of God? if they knew that Brigham Young was a prophet? and herself responded to the last question, "No, he is not a prophet of God. You have gone as far as the Lord wants you to go. You had better stay here; but if you will go to Utah, God bless you. I know you are honest, but the time will come when you will wish that you had stayed here." S. F. Walker

—Samuel F. Walker, Letter to Joseph Smith III, September 23, 1869, "Correspondence," *Saints' Herald* 16, no. 9 (November 1, 1869): 278.

ROUTE FROM LIVERPOOL
TO
Great Salt Lake Valley
ILLUSTRATED

Route From Liverpool to Great Salt Lake Valley, Illustrated With Steel Engravings and Wood Cuts From Sketches.
Published by Franklin D. Richards, Liverpool, England, 1855.

During the summer of 1853, the Smiths hosted two rather unusual visitors. Frederick Hawkins Piercy (1830-1891) was an artist. He was traveling with James Linforth (1827-1899), an assistant editor of the *Millennial Star* from England. As the pair traveled from Liverpool, England, to the Great Salt Lake in Utah, Piercy kept a detailed narrative of the journey and documented the trip with sketches of sites and portrait sketches of significant individuals encountered along the route. While at Nauvoo he produced sketches of the Nauvoo Temple in ruin and Carthage Jail. He also completed five portrait sketches of the Smith family, including his well known depiction of Lucy. After returning to England in 1854, Piercy's sketches were converted into high quality steel engravings by Charles Fenn. Editor Linforth attractively combined Piercy's narrative and sketches and produced a historical Mormon literary masterpiece. *Route from Liverpool to Great Salt Lake Valley, Illustrated with Steel Engravings and Wood Cuts from Sketches Made by Frederick Piercy*, published by Franklin D. Richards, originally appeared in fifteen separate issues from July 1854 to September 1855. Each issue in the series was covered with a separate green printed wrapper. Many sets of the work subsequently bound in England and shipped to Utah got wet and were damaged in transit. Consequently, the work is rather rare.

Frederick Hawkins Piercy

Frederick Piercy described his visit with Lucy:

WHILE IN NAUVOO I lodged at the Nauvoo Mansion formerly the residence of Joseph Smith, and now occupied by his mother, his widow and her family. I could not fail to regard the Old lady with great interest. Considering her age and afflictions, she at that time, retained her faculties to a remarkable degree. She spoke very freely of her sons, and with tears in her eyes, and every other symptom of earnestness, vindicated their reputations for virtue and truth. During my two visits I was able to take her portrait, and the portraits of two of her grandsons also, that of Joseph, the eldest son, was done on his 21st birth-day. He was born about 2 o'clock in the morning on the 6th of November, 1832, at Kirtland, Ohio. He is a young man of a most excellent disposition and considerable intelligence. One prominent trait in his character is his affection for his mother. I particularly noticed that his conduct towards her was always most respectful and attentive. The other portrait is of David, the youngest son, who was born 5 months after the assassination of his father.

He was born about 9 o'clock in the morning of the 17th of November, 1844. He is of a mild, studious disposition, and is passionately fond of drawing, seeming to be never so happy as when he has a pencil and paper in his hand. . . . I will say, that during some conversations which I had with persons in the neighborhood, I found that the whole family had obtained a most excellent reputation for integrity and industry.

–James Linforth, ed., *Route from Liverpool to Great Salt Lake Valley, Illustrated with Steel Engravings and Wood Cuts from Sketches Made by Frederick Piercy* . . . (Liverpool: Franklin D. Richards, 1855), 63-66.

Artist Piercy depictes himself while visiting the Carthage Jail, 1853.

A Contemporary Biography

Route from Liverpool to Great Salt Lake Valley, Illustrated with Steel Engravings

James Linforth edited the narrative, added footnotes, and inserted a contemporaneous biography of Lucy:

LUCY SMITH, MOTHER of the Prophet Joseph, was the daughter of Solomon and Lydia Mack. She was born at Gilsum, Cheshire, New Hampshire, on the 8th of July, 1776 [1775], and was the youngest of 8 children—4 of whom were girls. Solomon Mack had just attained his majority when the war between France and England, which grew out of disputed N. American territory, was proclaimed. He entered the British army, and had 2 teams in the service of King George II., employed in carrying Gen. Abercrombie's baggage, and was present in 1758, at the engagement on the west side of Lake George. He was engaged more or less in military pursuits until 1759, when he was discharged, and married an accomplished school teacher, Lydia Gates, the mother of the subject of this memoir. She was the daughter of Nathan Gates, a wealthy man, living in East Haddam, Conn. She was of a truly pious disposition, and had an excellent education, which particularly fitted her for the duties of a preceptress to her children, especially at a period when schools were rarities in the half cleared and thinly settled districts. Lucy profited by the talents and virtues of her mother. On the 24th of Jan., 1796, she was married to Joseph Smith, and received from her brother, Stephen Mack, and John Mudget, his partner, in business, a marriage present of 1000 dollars. Her husband owned a good farm at Tunbridge, on which they settled. The fruits of this marriage were 7 sons—Alvin, Hyrum, Joseph, Samuel H., Ephraim, William and Don Carlos; and 3 daughters—Sophronia, Catherine and Lucy. All the sons except William are now dead.

In 1802, Lucy Smith, with her husband, moved to Randolph, Vermont, where they opened a mercantile establishment. Mr. Smith here embarked in an adventure of gensang [sic], to China, but was robbed of the proceeds, and was

Lucy Mack Smith, engraving based on drawing by Frederick Piercy, 1853, *Route from Liverpool to Great Salt Lake Valley*.

much involved thereby. To liquidate his debts, he had to sell his farm at Tunbridge, to which he had then returned, and to use his wife's marriage present, which till then had remained untouched. From Tunbridge they removed to Royalton. They remained there a few months, and then went to reside at Sharon, Windsor County, where Joseph the Prophet was born. They again returned to Tunbridge and Royalton successively, but, in 1811, their circumstances having much improved, they quitted Vermont for Lebanon, in New Hampshire. Here their children were all seized with the typhus fever, though none fatally, and Joseph was afflicted with a fever sore. When health was restored to the family their circumstances were very low, and they returned to Vermont, and began to farm in Norwich. The first 2 years the crops failed, and the third the frost destroyed them, which determined Mr. Smith to remove to the State of New York. His wife and family did not remove until he had made preparations for them in Palmyra. Here the whole family set themselves industriously to repair their losses—Mr. Smith and his sons to farming, and Mrs. Smith to painting oil cloth coverings for tables, and were so prospered that in 2 years they were comfortably situated. After 4 years had elapsed, they removed to Manchester. In these alternate scenes of adversity and prosperity, the subject of religion was a constant theme with both Mr. and Mrs. Smith, though the former never subscribed to any particular sect. Both were occasionally favoured of the Lord with dreams or visions of the approaching work which He was about to commence on the earth, which prepared them for the mission of their son Joseph, and the

important part they were destined to take in it. Lucy Smith and several of her children joined the Presbyterian body, in the year 1819, but after Joseph had received the first visitation of the angel, and communicated the matter to his parents, she manifested intense interest in it, and from that time her history became identified with the mission of her son. She and her husband were baptized in April, 1830, and she removed to Kirtland, Ohio, in 1831, with the first company of Saints, where she rejoined her husband who had previously gone there in company with his son Joseph. Mr. Smith was several times torn from his wife by the enemies of the Saints, and unjustly imprisoned, but she manifested on all such occasions, a calm assurance that all would end well.

In 1838, all the family set out for Far West, a tedious and unpleasant journey, mostly through an unsettled country. They remained in Missouri until the extermination of the Saints from the State, participating in their numerous trials. On the occasion of the last arrest of her sons Joseph and Hyrum in that State, by the mob, in Oct., 1838, and when a court martial had decided to shoot them and others, she and her husband could distinctly hear the horrid yellings of the mob, which was encamped at a short distance from

DESERET NEWS.

Truth and Liberty.

VOL. 4.| GREAT SALT LAKE CITY, U.T., THURSDAY, NOV. 16, 1854. |NO. 36.

In 14 Monthly Parts, Royal Quarto, at 40 Cents each.

ROUTE FROM LIVERPOOL
TO
Great Salt Lake Valley:
ILLUSTRATED,

By a Series of splendid STEEL ENGRAVINGS and WOOD CUTS, from Sketches made on the spot from Life, in 1853, expressly for this Work, by

FREDERICK PIERCY,
AND CONTAINING A MAP OF THE OVERLAND PORTION OF THE JOURNEY.

EDITED BY JAMES LINFORTH.

This highly interesting and beautiful Work will form a narrative of the Journey from Liverpool to Great Salt Lake Valley, and will give Historical, Descriptive, and statistical information respecting the places, and the Indian Tribes on the route, and in Utah Territory.

The mode in which the Latter Day Saints' emigration is conducted; a review of it from the commencement; and incidental instructions to emigrants, will constitute an early part of the Work.

The Statistical information will be drawn from the most authentic sources, and consequently may be relied upon. That portion of it which relates to the Latter Day Saints, will be particularly valuable, owing to the difficulty hitherto experienced by all classes in obtaining anything accurate, from the conflicting statements which have appeared from time to time, in a great portion of the public press.

The engravings (except the Portraits of Joseph Smith, Heber C. Kimball, Willard Richards, Jedediah M. Grant, and John Smith; and Joseph Walker and Arapeen, Chiefs of the Utah Indians) are all taken from sketches made on the spot and from life, expressly for this Work, and will be finished in the first style of art, presenting a detail and an accuracy rarely aimed at in similar productions.

No pains or expense has been spared to render this Work one of peculiar interest, usefulness, and beauty; and the Publisher feels confident that it will meet with that extensive patronage which can alone justify its publication.

Steel Engravings by Charles Fenn, and Edwin Roffe:

New Orleans;
Baton Rouge;
Natchez under the Hill;
Natchez on the Hill;
Vicksburgh;
Memphis;
St. Louis;
Camp at Keokuk;
Nauvoo;
Joseph Smith, the Prophet;
Hyrum Smith, from an original portrait in the possession of his family;
Willard Richards, from a daguerreotype;
John Taylor;
Carthage Jail;
Room in which Joseph and Hyrum Smith were imprisoned;
Well against which Joseph Smith was placed and shot at after his assassination;
Lucy Smith, Mother of the Prophet;
Ruins of the Temple at Nauvoo;
Joseph Smith, jr., } Sons of the Prophet;
David Smith, }

Entrance to Kanesville;
Council Bluffs Ferry, and group of cottonwood trees;
View of the Missouri River, and Council Bluffs, from an elevation;
Elk Horn River Ferry;
Loup Fork Ferry;
Wood River;
Chimney Rock;
Scott's Bluffs;
Fort Laramie;
Independence Rock;
Devil's Gate;
Laramie Peak;
Witches' Bluff;
Great Salt Lake;
Great Salt Lake City;
Heber C. Kimball, from a daguerreotype;
Jedediah M. Grant,   ditto
John Smith,   ditto
President Brigham Young, also Governor of Utah Territory.

Wood Cuts by Mason Jackson:

Emigrant ship leaving Liverpool;
Light-House at the mouth of the Mississippi;
Old Fort Rosalie;
Walnut Hills;
Utah Territorial House, G. S. L. City;
Costume for the Plains;
Chimney Rock from the West;

Fort Bridger;
A Kanyon in the Rocky Mountains;
Tabernacle, G. S. L. City;
Joseph Walker, and
Arrapeen, brothers, and Chiefs of the Utah Indians, from original drawings by W. W. Major.

The First No. of the above Work was published in Liverpool by Elder F. D. Richards, in July last, and will be continued monthly until complete.

☞Persons wishing to obtain them, by applying to Elder S. W. Richards, 14th Ward, can have them free of carriage, at the above rate *paid in advance*. Immediate application should be made in order that they may be forwarded with the next Spring's Emigration.

A specimen number can be seen at Elder Richards' house.

37-3t

This ad for *Route From Liverpool to Great Salt Lake Valley* appeared in the November 23, 1854, edition of the *Deseret News*, Salt Lake City, Utah, page 3.

their house. Several guns were fired, and the heart-broken parent supposed the bloody work was accomplished. Mother Smith describes these moments—"Mr. Smith, folding his arms tight across his heart, cried out, 'Oh, my God! my God! they have killed my son! they have murdered him! and I must die, for I cannot live without him!' I had no word of consolation to give him, for my heart was broken within me—my agony was unutterable. I assisted him to the bed, and he fell back upon it helpless as a child, for he had not strength to stand upon his feet. The shrieking continued; no tongue can describe the sound which was conveyed to our ears; no heart can imagine the sensations of our breasts, as we listened to those awful screams. Had the army been composed of so many blood-hounds, wolves and panthers, they could not have made a sound more terrible." As the reader is aware, Joseph and Hyrum were not shot at that time, but were carried to Richmond, and thence to Liberty. At their departure from Far West, the heart-stricken mother pressed through the crowd to the wagon containing her sons, exclaiming—"I am the mother of the Prophet—is there not a gentleman here, who will assist me to that wagon, that I may take a last look at my children, and speak to them once

more before I die?" With her daughter Lucy, she gained the wagon, and grasped Joseph's hand, which was thrust between the cover and the wagon-bed, but he spoke not to her until she said—"Joseph, do speak to your poor mother once more, I cannot bear to go till I hear your voice." At this he sobbed out—"God bless you, mother;" and while his sister Lucy was pressing a kiss on his hand, the wagon dashed off. Mourning and lamentation now filled the old lady's breast, "but," says she, "in the midst of it I found consolation that surpassed all earthly comfort. I was filled with the Spirit of God." Shortly after this, Mr. Smith removed his family to Quincy, Illinois, to which place most of the Saints had previously fled, and in common with them suffered the hardships and privations which characterized the extermination from Missouri. From Quincy the family moved to Commerce, (Nauvoo), and on the 14th of Sept., 1840, Mr. Smith, after blessing his children individually, closed his earthly career. Mother Smith felt this bereavement keenly. . . . She had reared 6 sons to manhood, and only one remained, and he was at a distance from Nauvoo. Not one was near to console her in this trying hour. Some time after, she completed a very interesting little work, which she had for some time been preparing, entitled "Biographical Sketches of Joseph Smith the Prophet, and his Progenitors for Many Generations," which has since been published.

At the last General conference in Nauvoo, Mother Smith was permitted to address the Saints. She reviewed the scenes through which her sons and the church had passed, exhorted parents to exercise a proper care over the welfare of their children, and she expressed her intention to accompany the Saints into the wilderness, and requested that her bones after her death, should be brought back and be deposited in Nauvoo with her husband's, which President Young, and the whole conference, by vote, promised should be done. She had not, however, gone to Utah in 1853, but was living at the Nauvoo mansion with Emma Smith, where our Artist found her, and made the sketch for the portrait which we give of this venerable and extraordinary woman.

–James Linforth, ed., *Route from Liverpool to Great Salt Lake Valley, Illustrated with Steel Engravings and Wood Cuts from Sketches Made by Frederick Piercy . . .* (Liverpool: Published by Franklin D. Richards, 1855), 69-71.

The image in this *carte de visite* appears to be a photograph of a Daguerreian button. Such buttons were worn in remembrance during mourning. The image on this photograph is believed to be Lucy Mack Smith. Unfortunately the pictured button Daguerreotype is no longer extant and the image is preserved only in photographic form. See Ronald E. Romig and Lachlan Mackay, "Lucy's Image: A Recently Discovered Photograph of Lucy Mack Smith," *Journal of Mormon History* 31, no. 3 (Fall 2005): 61-77.

Lucy Mack Smith photograph, 1850s.

Horace S. Eldredge

Horace Eldredge.

Eldredge, who managed the LDS emigration system for several years, boarded at the Mansion, on July 28, 1853. His afternoon stroll around the city afforded:

❝**T**HE MOST peculiar feelings that ever I had while walking those streets." Contrast with former days of "gayety and pleasure and the Marks of industry and perseverance" by "a once happy people" who followed "principals of eternal truth" from a fallen leader at the hands of "a rough uncouth profane aspirant."

Emma was chilly to him. Of Lucy he noted, "The old lady seemed to know me and was verry much pleased to See me, and made many enquiries about Hyrum & Samuel Smiths families who are in the Valley. . . Mother Smith seemed to retain her recollection verry well of things that had transpired several years since. She wished me to remember her to many or all of her friends in the valley. I handed her $5.00 and took my leave of her for that time.

–Horace Sunderlin Eldredge, 1840-46 diary, Holograph, MS 1210, LDS Church Library.

Publication *of* Lucy's History

Lucy's receipt of a letter from Orson Pratt occasioned more than a little unanticipated pleasure. The Twelve had promised Lucy they would publish her manuscript history. At some point, Lucy turned her manuscript over to someone else. Soon after, Almon W. Babbitt, the Twelve's agent, bought it. Before Orson Pratt left the United States on a mission to England, he obtained the manuscript from Babbitt, with the intent of publishing it on the Church's press in Liverpool. Pratt wrote to Lucy in 1853 in hopes she would sell him the work's U.S. copyright.

Washington, D.C.
October 26, 1853

DEAR MOTHER Smith;— Last winter I purchased from A. W. Babbitt some manuscript relating to the early life of Joseph, the Prophet with the intention of publishing the same in England. The work is printed and bound and ready for sale in England. As the work has cost me between two and three thousand dollars in order to get the same before the public I should like very much to have the privilege of printing it in America: but as the work is issued in your name, and as you hold the copyright for this country, I have no right to publish it in the States, unless you should grant me that privilege. As soon as I can obtain a few of the best bound copies from England I will send them by mail to you.

I will also, as soon as I can obtain the means, send you one hundred dollars as a present. Brother Babbitt said to me that you were willing to sell me the copyright for $100. I will send you that amount as a present, and if you feel disposed to let me have the copyright as a present in return it will be thankfully received; if not you shall still be welcome to the $100; and I wish I was able to give you still more; but I am poor and my circumstances will not admit of it at present.

Perhaps I May at some future time have it in my power to help you still more. If you feel willing to grant me the copyright, I should be happy to receive a written document to that effect.

The Book of Mormon and Book of Covenants are already translated into several foreign languages and the great work of the Lord of which your son was the honored instrument in bringing forth, is spreading rapidly into the four quarters of the globe.

Oh, Mother Smith, how often do I think of those happy days, when I had the joyful privilege of coming under your roof in Waterloo, N.Y. I have been your true friend from that day to this, although I am sorry to say, I have not been as faithful in all things as I might have been; I greatly appreciated the society of the Prophet while living; but I ought to have appreciated him still more: and could I have my life to live over again in his precious society I think, with the experience that I now have, that I never could do enough for his happiness and welfare.

It would afford me much pleasure to place my eyes once more upon his aged and venerable mother, but circumstances may never grant me that privilege in this life. May the Lord bless you, dear mother, and in His own good time receive you into those happy mansions where dwell your dear children, and when I have finished my work may the Lord grant me the privilege of coming there too.

I subscribe myself your humble servant for Christ's sake.

Orson Pratt

P.S. Please remember my kind love to all your dear children that are living, and to your grandchildren; and also to sister Emma. May God remember his promise to them and bless them all.

–Orson Pratt, Washington, D. C., Letter to Lucy Mack Smith, October 26, 1853, Typescript, P70-1, f16, CofC Archives.

Lucy happily replied to Orson's letter. In January 1854, Orson answered Lucy's letter announcing that he was sending her ten presentation copies of the new work.

Lucy's history, presentation binding.

Orson Pratt

Washington City, D.C.
January 16th 1854

MRS. LUCY SMITH
I have just received your
letter of Nov <Dec> 20th.
Absence prevented me from receiving it before. Since I wrote to you
I have received a few copies of the
"Biographical Sketches" &c which I
got printed in England. I had a few
copies printed on Superior paper,
and bound in Morocco extra and
nicely gilted. I send you ten of these
by the same mail with this letter.
I have prepaid the postage on the
same. I purchased the manuscripts
of A. W. Babbitt: he told me that he
purchased the same from some man
in Cincinnati at an expense of several hundred dollars. It was at Washington that I purchased them. Mr.
Babbitt, after he sold them to me,
visited Nauvoo, and on his return
to Washington, he stated, as near
as I could <can> recollect, that you
would Sell the title for this country
for $100. I did not particularly wish
to purchase the title at that time,
and told him that I would make you
a present of $100 dollars, and you
could do as you saw proper about
giving me the title. I have advertized [sic] the books for sale, but as
yet there is no demand for them. I
am doubtful whether one hundred
dollars worth could be sold to the
world in the United States in ten
years. Moreover, if the books were
saleable, I am not at present in circumstances to print them in this
country. When I wrote to you last
my prospects were somewhat better than at present. I think if you
could get some one that had means
to print two or three thousand, and
transport them to Utah, they would
sell in the course of a few years. I
consider it to be a very interesting
volume, and one which every good
saint will highly esteem. I have on
hand in this country about 20 or
thirty copies of the common binding, and a very few of the best bound
ones, such as I have forwarded to
you. I do not think that I will have
any need to bring any more from
England. Those that I had in England are now out of my hands, and
I will have to purchase all that I get
the same as I did the few copies that
I now have.

You inquire of me, if I am in the
possession of the Book of blessings
of father Smith; I am not. I have not
manuscripts or copies of any kind,
excepting my own composition, neither am I able to tell you any thing
in relation to them. I can not call to
mind that I have ever seen them for
many years. I will in a few days if the
Lord permits, send you a check or

Orson Pratt published Lucy's manuscript in England, 1853.

draft for $100. I wish I were able to help you more, but I am poor, and considerably in debt, and my own family are in needy circumstances. But I shall ever feel a near and sacred tie to every branch of the Smith family who have been the means in the hands of God, of bringing salvation to me and to this generation if they will receive it. I may, at some future time, be in better circumstances, when, if God spares your

life, I shall take pleasure in assisting you. I remember the kindness and hospitality received at your house in Waterloo, N. York, and also in Kirtland; I also remember with gratitude the kindness which I received at the hands of Sister Emma, when I received a home under her hospitable roof in Kirtland. Many times when returning from my missions, weary and foot sore, I have been welcomed, as if under my own father's roof. May God bless you, mother Smith, and your generations after you forever and ever. Great are the promises of the Lord in the Book of Covenants to your descendants, and I long, with much desire, for the time to come, when I shall see them in the midst of Zion, armed with righteousness, and with the power of God in great glory. Every honest, true, humble soul, would rejoice exceedingly to see you, and your descendants & your kindred in their midst. Shall we be thus highly favored? Give my kind respects to sister Emma, and to all your grand children. I should be highly gratified to visit you before I return to Utah, but I do not know as I shall be able to do so. Will you be so kind as to have Joseph your grand son return me a line immediately upon the reception of the books; that I may know whether they come safely. Permit me to subscribe myself your most humble and sincere friend for Christ sake.

Orson Pratt.

–Orson Pratt, Washington City, D. C., Letter to Lucy Mack Smith, January 16, 1854, Miscellany, P19, f24, CofC Archives.

LITERARY NOTICE.

BIOGRAPHICAL SKETCHES of Joseph Smith, the Prophet, and his progenitors for many generations: by Lucy Smith, mother of the Prophet.

 THIS NEW and highly interesting work should be possessed by all Saints who feel in the least degree interested with the history of the latter day work. Many facts which it contains, and never before published, are of great importance to the world, and the work constitutes a valuable acquisition to the libraries of the Saints.

The above named work can be obtained from S. W. Richards, 14th Ward; Joseph Cain, at the post office, J. M Horner's Co., Deseret Store; and may be ordered through the agents for the Deseret News, generally throughout the Territory. Price $1.75.

–*Deseret News* 4, no. 36 (November 16, 1854): 3.

John Lyman Smith

Lucy's nephew, John Lyman Smith, recorded his visit with his aunt on Monday, July 2, 1855, in his journal. John observed,

AUNT LUCY HAD BEEN confined to the bed for 10 months unable to walk with the rheumatism.

–John Lyman Smith, Journal, July 2, 1855, Holograph, MS 1122. LDS Church Library.

Enoch Tripp

In November 1855, Enoch Tripp found Lucy Mack Smith

LIVING IN A LONELY room in the eastern part of the house; she was . . . very feeble. . . . She arose in bed and placing her hands around my neck, kissed me exclaiming, "I can now die in peace since I have beheld your face from the valleys of the mountains."

–Journal of Enoch B. Tripp, November 25, 1855; cited in Newell and Avery, *Mormon Enigma*, 265.

Wilford Woodruff once described a sermon by Tripp that represented Lucy as having

CLASPED HIM IN HER arms (they were formerly acquainted) & she said My son Enoch I am glad to again see you. I am glad to see a man again from Salt Lake. She cryed for Joy, and said she had desired for two years to be with the saints in the vallies of the Mountains but others had hindered her. She alluded to Emma. She says give my love to Brigham & Heber & all the faithful saints for my heart is with them.

–*Woodruff's Journal*, September 7, 1856, 4:445.

When Lucy could no longer walk Lewis [Bidamon] built a wheelchair for her. Finally Lucy's arthritic hands became so drawn out of shape that she was unable to feed herself. In spite of the difficulties Emma arranged for Lucy to move in with Joseph Smith III's family on the Smith farm several miles southeast of Nauvoo.

–Newell and Avery, *Mormon Enigma*, 265.

The shafts slide under the seat until the back of the chair rests against the axle of the wheels. Lifting the shafts raise the chair. In this way an invalid can be rolled through yards and gardens with very little effort. –Catharine Esther Beecher, *Miss Beecher's Domestic Receipt Book: Designed as a Supplement to Her Treatise on Domestic Economy* (New York: Harper, 1850), 216.

In 1855, Joseph Smith III studied law in Canton, Illinois. Upon his homecoming he married Emeline Griswold and the couple moved to the family farm. As the end of Lucy's life quickly approached, Joseph III moved his grandmother to the farm, about two miles southeast of town, where he and his wife Emeline could provide her with constant care. Elizabeth Pilkington, the young daughter of a neighbouring farmer, also helped nurse Lucy during her final days.

–Edward Tullidge, *Life of Joseph the Prophet* (Plano, Illinois: RLDS Board of Publication, 1880), 759.

On May 4, 1856, Joseph [III] corresponded with his friend Emma Knight, noting, "Grandmother is not very well at present. We are afraid she cannot last much longer."

–Joseph Smith III, Letter to Emma Knight, May 4, 1856, Knight Family Papers, USHS.

Lucy's Death

Ten days later, on Wednesday, May 14, 1856, Lucy Mack Smith died at age eighty-one. The next day Lucy's remains were returned to town where she was buried behind the Smith family homestead at Nauvoo, near her husband.

–A Book of Mormons, 312.

Though probably not accurate, Vida Smith, daughter of Alexander H. Smith, suggests that Lucy died in the sitting room on the southeast corner of the Mansion House main floor.

ERE THE aged mother of Joseph, the Martyr, Grandma Lucy Mack Smith, spent some of the last days of her life; and here, I am informed, she died.

–Vida E. Smith, "A Historic Trio.–No. 2," *Autumn Leaves* 16, no. 4 (April 1906): 152.

Joseph III advised family friend John Bernhisel by letter of Lucy's passing.

RANDMA DIED THE morning of the 14th of May last easily and with her senses to the last moment and we trust she has no wish to return from the "bourne." She appeared somewhat fearful of death at a little while before he came yet appeared resigned afterwards.

I sat by her and held her hand in mine till death relived her—the first death scene I ever witnessed—Long may I be spared the death scene of my mother.

–Joseph Smith III, Letter to John Bernhisel; quoted in Anderson, *Lucy's Book*, 796.

John Bernhisel.

George A. Smith prepared an eulogy for Lucy that appeared in the *Millennial Star*.

WHEN THE SAINTS resolved to leave Nauvoo for the Rocky Mountains, she addressed a general conference, bearing testimony of the truth, and of her desire to lay her bones in Nauvoo beside her husband and sons. ... She enjoyed the gifts and influence of the Holy Spirit much. Blessed woman! Her name and memory are engraven upon the tablets of the hearts of tens of thousands, and will be handed down to millions yet unborn, who will speak her praise and talk of her virtues and goodness, of her motherly kindness, her watchful care and administration to the sick and afflicted—the kind and affectionate mother, the beloved wife, the partner of her aged and venerable husband—of her deeds of love, her virtue, faith, hope, and confidence in her God, the trials and persecutions she bore for the Gospel of truth, her unvarying steadfastness to truth through all circumstances; and being filled with charity to all, her God blessed her, and nerved her up to bear the persecutions and trials she was called upon to undergo, and gave her strength and grace sufficient for her day, and, in copious profusion, poured out His Holy Spirit upon her. . . . But her labors are closed, and like a shock of corn fully ripe, she has gone down to her grave in peace, full of honor and goodness, to await the morning of the first resurrection, after having lived to commit to the silent tomb, her husband, Joseph, Hyrum, Don Carlos, Samuel, &c. . . . Peace to her ashes. G. A. Smith

–George A. Smith, Lucy Mack Smith, Obituary, *Millennial Star* 18, no. 35 (August 30, 1856): 559-60.

Following Lucy's death, showman A. Combs came to finalize his purchase of the Egyptian mummies.

Nauvoo City May 25/56
THIS CERTIFIES THAT we have sold to; Mr. A Combs four Egyptian Mummies with the records of them. These Mummies were obtained from the catacombs of Egypt sixty feet below the surface of the Earth, by the antiquarian society of Paris & forwarded to New York & purchased by the Mormon Prophet Joseph Smith at the price of twenty four hundred dollars in the year Eighteen hundred thirty-five they were highly prized by Mr. Smith on account of the importance which attached to the records which were accidentally

Woman to the right standing near Lucy's grave in Smith family burial yard, photo by G. E. Anderson, 1907, courtesy Church Archives, The Church of Jesus Christ of Latter-day Saints.

found enclosed in the breast of one of the Mummies. From translation by Mr. Smith of the Records these Mummies were found to be the family of Pharaoh King of Egypt. They were kept exclusively by Mr. Smith until his death & since by the Mother of Mr. Smith notwithstanding we have had repeated offers to purchase which have invariably been refused until her death which occurred on the fourteenth of this month.

L. C. Bidamon
Emma Bidamon:
former wife of Jos. Smith
Joseph Smith III
Nauvoo, Hancock Co. Ill
May 26 [1856]

—Certificate of sale of mummies and records, signed by L.C. and Emma Bidamon, and Joseph Smith III, Typescript, P5, f69, CoC Archives.

This bill of sale was published in the *Daily Missouri Democrat* in June 1857, suggesting that A. Combs resold the Mormon Egyptana and furnished whoever purchased them with a copy of his original bill of sale.

—Stanley B. Kimball, "New Light on Old Egyptana" *Dialogue*

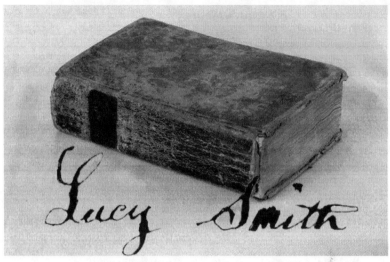

Joseph III inherited Lucy's Book of Mormon.

Withdrawal of Lucy's History

After Lucy's history appeared, Brigham Young stated that he wished the book to be revised and corrected. Wilford Woodruff noted in his journal:

HE WISHED US TO take up that work & revise it & Correct it that it belonged to the Historians to attend to it that there was many fals[e] statements made in it and he wished them to be left out and all other statements which we did not know to be true, and give the reason why they are left out. G. A. Smith & Elias Smith should be present [to do it]. That

Book makes out William Smith according to Mother Smith's statement to be full of the Holy Ghost & the power of God.

– Woodruff's Journal, February 13, 1859, 5: 287.

Orson Pratt attempted to accommodate Brigham's concerns, initially hopeful he would be able to continue to offer Lucy's book for sale. In the end, it was withdrawn from the market.

A BRIEF SKETCH

Of the History of Joseph Smith the Prophet, and of his progenitors, written by his Mother, Lucy Smith.

This work was first published in England, in 1853. I procured the manuscripts while on my last mission in the United States, and was informed, at the time, that most of the work was written under the inspection of the Prophet; but from evidences since received, it is believed that the greater part of the manuscripts did not pass under his review, as there are items which are ascertained to be incorrect.

These imperfections have undoubtedly arisen either from the impaired memory of the highly respected and aged authoress, or from the lack of correct information; or, which is the most probable, from the carelessness of the scribe in writing from time to time isolated statements from her mouth without a sufficient understanding of their connection.

In future editions the work will be carefully revised and corrected so far as we have knowledge. In the meantime, it is believed that this history will be interesting to the Saints, and to the public generally, as from it they can make themselves acquainted with some of the greatest and most remarkable events of modern times.

If the schools of onr Territory would introduce this work as a "Reader," it would give the young and rising generation some knowledge of the facts and incidents connected with the opening of the grand dispensation of the last days.   ORSON PRATT, Sen.

[Papers published oy the Latter Day Saints will please copy.]

Notice by Orson Pratt in response to Brigham's Young's concern about Lucy's history.,
Deseret News 5, no. 2 (March 21, 1855): 8.

RLDS member Thomas Job advised Joseph III of Brigham's Young's treatment of Lucy's history.

Salt Lake City, Aug. 24, 1868.

BROTHER Joseph Smith: Brigham Young lately traversed every settlement in the Territory, collecting up all the copies of the *Biographical Sketches of Joseph Smith the Prophet and his Progenitors*, by Mother Lucy Smith. He said that they are nothing but falsehoods, that there were "more lies in them than Lucifer ever told," that he was going to grind these books over again. But the chief cause is (as one observed) that that book gives a little more favorable account of Sister Emma than Brigham Young does. His exertion is to hurry that family into oblivion, if possible. His wrath towards that family is without bounds. Brigham would also grind the Book of Doctrine and Covenants over again, if there was any chance at all to do it. One thing I am certain of, that another edition of that book will never be issued by the Brighamites, no; not even if they were to hold their position for a thousand years.

– Thomas Job, Letter to Joseph Smith III, "From Bro. Thomas Job," *Herald* 14, no. 6 (September 15, 1868): 91.

Publication History

Lucy's history was first published in Liverpool, England, for Orson Pratt by Samuel W. Richards in 1853, under the title: *Biographical Sketches of Joseph Smith the Prophet, and His Progenitors for Many Generations.* Lucy's work turned out to be as much an autobiography of Lucy as a biography of Joseph Smith.

In 1865 in Utah, Brigham Young recalled *Biographical Sketches* because of assumed inaccuracies. George A. Smith and Elias Smith produced a revision of the 1853 text published in 1902 containing an introduction by Joseph F. Smith. It did not indicate where the text had been altered nor the reason. The 1902 edition was further edited with notes and comments by Preston Nibley in 1945 and published by Bookcraft of Salt Lake City under the title *History of Joseph Smith By His Mother, Lucy Mack Smith.*

The Reorganized Church of Jesus Christ of Latter Day Saints published editions of Lucy's book based on the original 1853 publication in 1880 and 1908 as *Biographical Sketches of Joseph Smith the Prophet, and His Progenitors for Many Generations.* It was republished again by the Reorganization in 1912 with notes by Church Historian He-man C. Smith. Modern Microfilm Co., Salt Lake City, issued a repro-duction of the 1853 first edition in 1965 with an introduction by Jerald and Sandra Tanner. RLDS Herald Publishing House in Independence, Missouri, issued a paperback version of this edition in 1969. And Arno Press and the New York Times pub-lished another printing in 1969.

–Marquardt & Walters, *Invent-ing Mormonism*, 221-22.

Recently, several scholars have sought to recover the con-tent of Lucy's original draft:

–Lavina Fielding Anderson, *Lu-cy's Book: A Critical Edition of Lucy Mack Smith's Family Memoir.*

–R. Vernon Ingleton, comp., *History of Joseph Smith by His Moth-er Lucy Mack Smith; the Unabridged Original Version.*

–Scot Facer Proctor and Mau-rine Jensen Proctor, eds., *The Re-vised and Enhanced History of Joseph Smith by His Mother.*

–Dan Vogel, "Lucy Smith His-tory," *Early Mormon Documents*, Vol. 1.

Edward Stevenson

Stevenson, an LDS member, reported visiting Lucy's grave.

September 26, 1895

BEFORE LEAVING [Nau-voo] we visited the lonely graves of Joseph Smith senior, his wife Lucy Mack Smith and the family's private burying ground, which is on the banks of the Mississippi—just north of the old homestead of the Prophet. The house on this [lot] is still standing and is owned by young Joseph, as we sometimes call him. It is occu-pied by a renter, who, after showing us through the low ceiling rooms of the early days of Nauvoo, pi-loted us to the graveyard. To our surprise only one slab marked the last resting place of the Smith fam-ily—a flat reclining slab of elaborate dimension on which is engraven: "Emma Smith Bidamon, born July 10th 1803. Died April 30th 1879." Still further north are three tombs the wife son and daughter of Joseph Smith, the grandson of he who lies with nothing but some lilac bushes to mark the spot of himself, his wife and his family.

–Edward Stevenson, "Steven-son's Travels," *The Deseret Weekly* 51, no. 17 (October 12, 1895), 21.

Marking Lucy's Grave

In 1867, Emma Bidamon expressed her desire to mark the graves of her in-laws, in a letter to Joseph Smith III.

JOSEPH I SHOULD LIKE if you are willing to extend that fence so as to enclose the graves of your two little brothers. I have got twenty five dollars that no one has any right to but myself. . . I feel anxious to apply that money on that graveyard, after I have done that I think I can ask our Smith relatives to help mark Fathers and Mothers graves if no more.

–Emma Smith Bidamon, Letter to Joseph Smith III, December 2, 1867, CofC Archives.

Emma's letter demonstrates that there was no lack of aspiration within the Smith family to appropriately mark loved ones' graves, especially the grave of Lucy. However, the many midwest Smiths' personal affiliations with the Reorganized Church limited their ability to act upon this desire. Emma, Joseph III, Alexander, and David H. each joined and supported the Reorganization in its infancy and all labored under great personal and financial sacrifice to aid its course. No resource could be reasonably spared as family members consistently suppressed personal needs in order to focus their resources on this developing institution. Also, in 1862, Joseph IIIs personally assumed his brother Frederick G. W.'s debts that had been accrued due to his unsuccessful effort to operate the Smith family farm southeast of Nauvoo while simultaneously battling a fatal disease. Joseph struggled financially throughout the remainder of his life.

Upon several occasions, both the family and the RLDS Church initiated efforts to appropriately commemorate those who had nobly sacrificed so much for the gospel. In 1891, following the death of Lewis Bidamon, Joseph and Alexander succeeded in erecting a modest marker upon the grave of their beloved mother who had died in 1879. The location of Lucy's grave, as well as those of others, became less certain with the passing of each generation. Later Smith generations continued to maintain this commemorative dream in various ways. Eventually, a wonderful collaboration among members of the extended

Smith family resulted in the erection of attractive marble stones over the graves of Lucy and Joseph Sr. and the other modern-day markers in the Smith Family Graveyard.

The Joseph Sr. and Lucy Mack Smith Family newsletter noted,

AT LAST, AFTER years of uncertainty, the resting places of both Joseph Smith Sr. and Lucy Mack Smith have been located and verified. The story is a veritable, high-tech Scotland Yard clue chase. The *Saints Herald* in 1950 published an account of the location of the Joseph Smith Sr. and Lucy Mack Smith graves. It was the account by the family cemetery sexton, [Mr. Kendall], who was shown the sites by the original grave digger who had buried Emeline, the wife of Joseph the 3rd in 1869. He had inadvertently disturbed Mother Smith's grave, and with the help of Emma, made identification. L. G. Holloway wrote:

"[It was] several years ago that I learned of the exact location of these [Joseph Smith Sr.'s and Lucy Mack Smith's] graves. In company with Mr. Kendall, a brother-in-law of Alexander Smith, I visited these burial grounds. He took me to the spot where Joseph and Lucy Smith are buried. It was identified at the time by a grave dug for Emmeline [Emeline] Smith [died 1869], first wife of Young Joseph, son of the Martyr. While digging, Mr. Kendall found another grave and took from it some of the articles in the casket. These articles he showed to Emma, wife of the Martyr, who said they had belonged to Lucy [died 1856] who was buried beside her companion [died 1840 and moved to the riverbank about 1846]. Mr. Kendall informed me that he did not disturb these graves but simply started digging the new one about four feet west. This grave [Emeline's] is clearly marked, so we have the identity of the last resting place of the father and mother of the prophet."

Emeline Smith, wife of Joseph III.

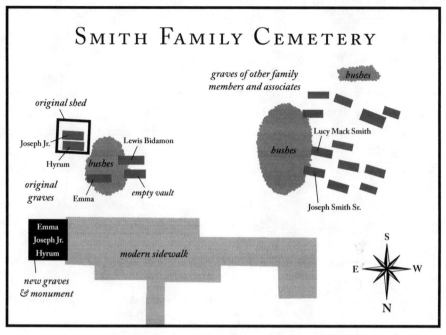

Smith family grave locations. Map by John Hamer.

–Leonard G. Holloway, *Saints' Herald* 97, no. 45 (November 6, 1950): 9.

We published this account in our newsletter with a request that anyone in the family with corroborating journal accounts to please inform us. Not long after, another sent us an account that contradicted the sexton's account, made by Joseph and Lucy's grandson. It was then decided to continue the sleuthing by using modern technology. It took some time for all the puzzle pieces to fit but now they do. After

some search and proper timing, a ground penetrating radar scan was arranged. Here are some excerpts from the final scan report.

"The x-ray [deep ground radar] images arise from variations in the soils caused by pit excavation and refilling. The overall uniformity of the soils in this cemetery indicates considerable coffin decay. . . . The considerable mixing of soils makes the identification of child burials particularly difficult, because of the smaller size. . . ."

The diagram shows four marked graves, including Emeline's that will serve as reference since the x-ray verified their currently marked positions. The investigative mystery was discovering whether there were graves either to the east or to the west of Emeline's as per the contradicting accounts. Now quoting again: "The area just west of Emeline is vacant. . . . Mother Smith could . . . be to the east of Emeline. The scan indicates that we do have a grave image in this eastern area that is close to Emeline and matches the *Saints' Herald* account by the cemetery sexton. There is also a grave image just to the side of the Lucy image [site] that must be Father Smith's.

–Joseph Sr. and Lucy Mack Smith Family Newsletter 11 (Fall 2001): 1; http://www.joseph-smithsr.org/documents/newsletter/NewsletterFall2001.pdf.

Radar survey findings, conducted by T. Michael Smith, a LDS Church staff archaeologist, supported the Holloway account, and the final resting places of Lucy Mack Smith and Joseph Smith Sr. were likely identified. With this information, The Community of Christ, The Church of Jesus Christ of Latter-day Saints, and the Joseph Smith Sr. and Lucy Mack Smith Family Foundation, continued a joint effort to finally mark the graves. "Smith relatives" responded generously, and during the spring of 2002, the brick walk in the Smith Family Graveyard was extended, and the graves of Lucy and Joseph marked.

–Lachlan Mackay, "A Brief History of the Smith Family Cemetery," *Mormon Historical Studies* 3, no. 2 (Fall 2002): 240-52.

Joseph Sr.'s and Lucy Mack Smith's marble gravestones.

SMITH FAMILY BURIAL GROUND, NAUVOO, ILLINOIS
[Generations are indented]

Joseph Smith, Sr. (1771-1840)
Lucy Mack Smith (1775-1856)

— Joseph Smith, Jr. 1805-1844)
Emma Smith (1804-1879)
— Frederick Granger Williams Smith (1836-1862)
— Don Carlos Smith (1840-1841)
— Stillborn Son (1842)
Emeline Griswold Smith (JIII's wife) (1838-1869)
— Evelyn R. Smith (Joseph III's dau.) (1859)
— Joseph Arthur Smith (JIII's son) (1865-1866)

— Hyrum Smith (1800-1844)
— Hyrum Smith Jr. (1834-1841)

— Samuel H. Smith (1808-1844)
Mary Bailey Smith (wife of Samuel) (1808-1841)
— Lucy B. Smith [probably buried here] (1841)
(Lucy is the daughter of Samuel and Mary)

— Don Carlos Smith (1816-1841)
— Sophronia C. Smith (dau. of Don Carlos) (1838-1843)

Caroline Grant Smith [probably buried here] (1814-1845)
— (Caroline is the wife of William B. Smith)

Others:
Lewis Crum Bidamon (1806-1891)
Celeste Gifford (1855-1856)
Edwin James Gifford (1863-1865)
Maude A. Gifford (1871)
Wilber W. Gifford (1853)
Robert B. Thompson (1811-1841)

The Venerable Lucy Smith:
by Miss Eliza R. Snow

She's followed to the grave five noble sons!
She stood beside the bleeding forms of those
Great brother-martyrs of the latter day. . . .
And yet she lives, and yet bears witness to
The truth for which they fell a sacrifice.
Yes, venerable lady, thou shalt live
While life to thee shall be a blessing. Thou
Art dear to every faithful Saint. Thousands
Already bless thee, millions yet to come
Will venerate thy name and speak they praise.

–Eliza R. Snow, *Times and Seasons* 6, no. 9 (May 15, 1845): 911.

Distinguished Women
by J. M. Holaday

This woman's last bright years, all calm with peace,
Were spent by waters clear, near heaven's plane;
And balmy was the hour of her release
From earthly ills and human hatred vain.
True servant of the Just, thy path of fire
Inclines my soul to shun the mortal state
And court the fair abode of mansions higher
With Lucy Smith, and Alvin pure and great.

–J. M. Holaday, in H. C. Smith, "Distinguished Women," *Journal of History* 12, no. 1 (January 1919): 106.

TO THE READING PUBLIC:

Lavina Fielding Anderson, "Epilogue: Lucy's Last Years," *Lucy's Book: A Critical Edition of Lucy Mack Smith's Family Memoir* (Salt Lake City, Utah: Signature Books, 2001).

Lavina Fielding Anderson, "Lucy Mack Smith," in Kyle R. Walker, ed., *United by Faith: The Joseph Sr. and Lucy Mack Smith Family* (American Fork, Utah: Covenant Communications, Inc., 2005), 40-80.

R. Vernon Ingleton, comp., *History of Joseph Smith by His Mother Lucy Mack Smith: The Unabridged Original Version* (Provo, Utah: Stratford Books, 2005).

Gracia N. Jones, *Lucy and Emma* (American Fork, Utah: Covenant Communications, Inc., 2005).

Lachlan Mackay, "A Brief History of the Smith Family Cemetery," *Mormon Historical Studies* 3, no. 2 (Fall 2002): 240-252.

Lisa J. Peck, *Lucy Mack Smith* (Mothers of the Prophets Series) (Springville, Utah: Cedar Fort, Inc., 2004).

Scot Facer Proctor and Maurine Jensen Proctor, eds., *The Revised and Enhanced History of Joseph Smith by His Mother* (Salt Lake City, Utah: Bookcraft, 1996).

Ronald Romig and Lachlan Mackay, "Lucy's Image: A Recently Discovered Photograph of Lucy Mack Smith," *Journal of Mormon History* 32, no. 3 (Fall 2005): 61-77.

Dan Vogel, "Lucy Mack Smith Collection," *Early Mormon Documents*, Vol. 1 (Salt Lake City, Utah: Signature Books, 1996), 227-450.

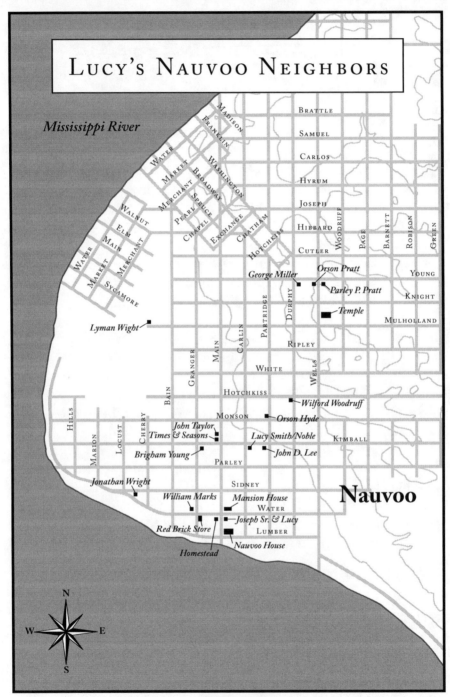

LUCY'S NAUVOO NEIGHBORS

Mississippi River

BRATTLE

SAMUEL

CARLOS

HYRUM

JOSEPH

MADISON

FRANKLIN

WASHINGTON

BROADWAY

SPRUCE

EXCHANGE

CHATHAM

HOTCHKISS

HIBBARD

CUTLER

WOODRUFF

PAGE

BARNETT

ROBISON

GREEN

WATER

MARKET

MERCHANT

PEARL

CHAPEL

George Miller ■

■ *Orson Pratt*

YOUNG

WALNUT

ELM

MAIN

MERCHANT

WATER

MARKET

SYCAMORE

■ *Parley P. Pratt*

KNIGHT

PARTRIDGE

DURPHY

■ *Temple*

MULHOLLAND

Lyman Wight ■

GRANGER

MAIN

CARLIN

RIPLEY

WHITE

WELLS

BAIN

HOTCHKISS

■ *Wilford Woodruff*

HILLS

MARION

LOCUST

CHERRY

MONSON

John Taylor
Times & Seasons ■

■ *Orson Hyde*

Lucy Smith/Noble

KIMBALL

Brigham Young ■

■ *John D. Lee*

PARLEY

Jonathan Wright ■

SIDNEY

William Marks ■

Mansion House ■

WATER

Nauvoo

Red Brick Store

■ *Joseph Sr. & Lucy*

LUMBER

Homestead

Nauvoo House

N
W   E
S

Map by John Hamer.

2782121

Made in the USA